Ivan Kushnir

Economy of Bermuda

Series "Economy in countries"

first published: 2019
last updated: 2021-01-26

Ivan Kushnir. Economy of Bermuda. Series "Economy in countries". - 2019. - 70 pages.

This book about the economy of Bermuda from the 1970s to the 2010s. Source data from UN Data.

Size. In the 2010s, the gross domestic product of Bermuda was equal to $6.8 billion per year; the value of agriculture was $18.7 million; the value of industry was $140.7 million. Since the share in the world is less than .01%, the country is classified as a micro economy.

Productivity. In the 2010s, the GDP per capita was $105 677.4, the value of agriculture per capita was $292.2, the value of industry per capita was $2 201.2. Since the productivity is greater the average above average, the economy is classified as high developed.

Growth. In the 2010s, the growth of gross domestic product was -0.66%; the growth of agriculture was -2.7%; the growth of industry was -5.2%.

Structure. In the 2010s, the economy of Bermuda included: services (78.7%), trade (10.1%), transportation (5.1%), construction (3.6%), industry (2.2%), and agriculture (0.29%).

Exports and imports. In the 2010s, the exports were 2.1 times higher than the imports, the net exports were equal to 26.3% of the GDP. The technological structure of exports are not better than the structure of imports.

Consumption and reproduction. The attitude of reproduction to the consumption is not better than the global average, so the share of GDP in the world will not increase.

Series "Economy in countries": parallel.page.link/en

ISBN: 9781794659841

Contents

Part I. Size

	The 2010s
GDP	$6.8 billion
The share in the world	0.0087%
Share in the Americas	0.027%
Share in Northern America	0.034%

Chapter I. Gross domestic product

The gross domestic product of Bermuda rose from $477.0 million per year in the 1970s to $6.8 billion per year in the 2010s, that is by $6.3 billion or 14.2 times. The change occurred at $5.8 billion due to a 7.1-fold increase in prices, as also at $399.4 million due to a 1.7-fold increase in productivity, as well as at $76.9 million due to the expansion in population. The average annual growth in GDP is 1.7%. The minimum value of gross domestic product was in 1970 at $265.5 million. The maximum value of GDP was in 2019 at $7.4 billion.

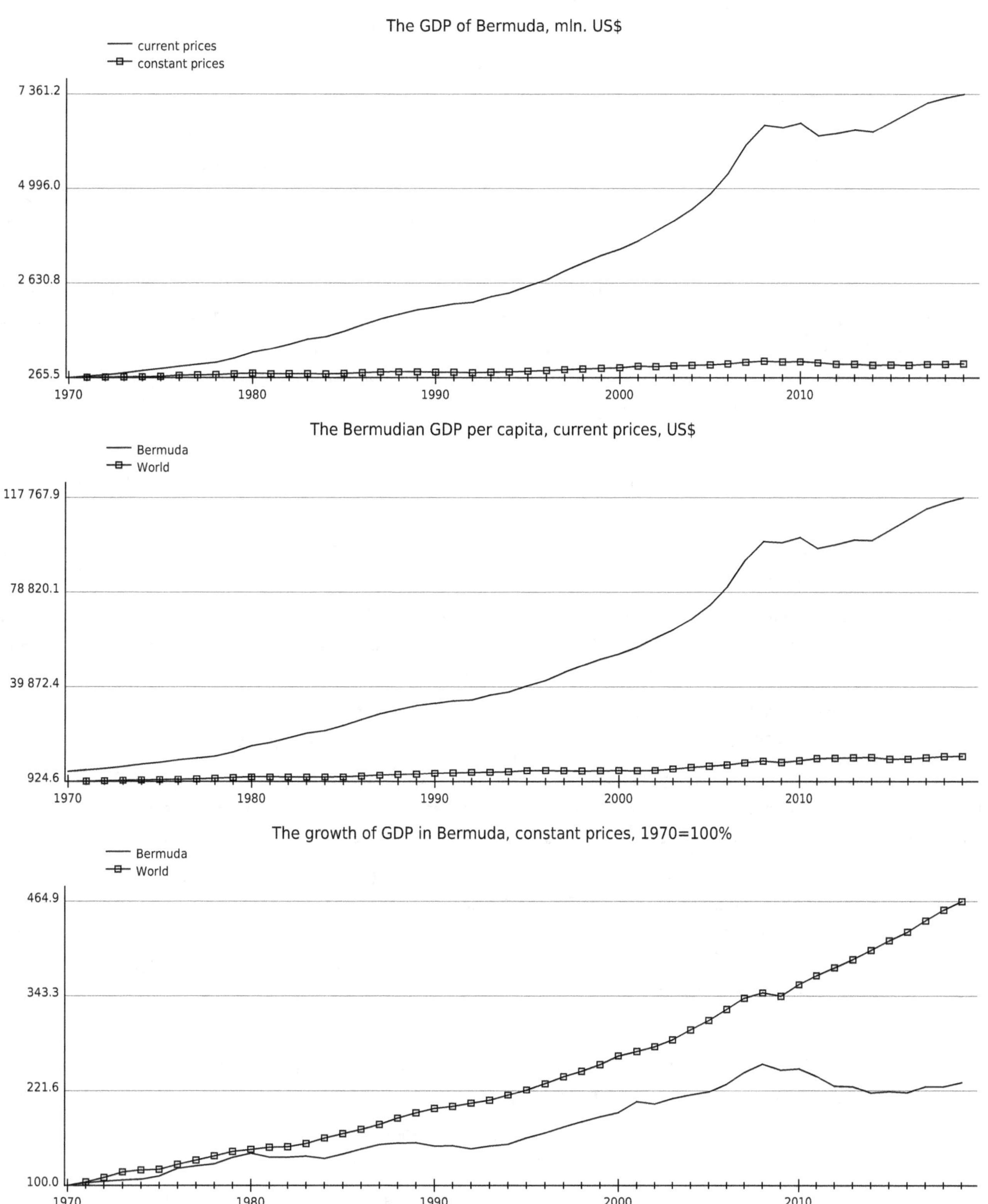

The GDP of Bermuda, mln. US$

The Bermudian GDP per capita, current prices, US$

The growth of GDP in Bermuda, constant prices, 1970=100%

The 1970s

The gross domestic product of Bermuda was $477.0 million per year in the 1970s, ranked 139th in the world. The share in the world was 0.0073%, and 0.021% in the Americas.

The gross domestic product of Bermuda consisted of: household expenditure (68.3%), capital formation (13.9%), government expenditure (9.8%), and net export (8.5%).

The Bermuda's GDP per capita was $8 668.2 in the 1970s, ranked 10th in the world, and was on a par with Andorra ($8.7 thousand). The Bermuda's GDP per capita was greater than gross domestic product per capita in the world ($1 620.8) in 5.3 times, and was greater than gross domestic product per capita in the Americas ($4 044.6) in 2.1 times.

The growth of GDP in Bermuda was 3.5% in the 1970s, ranked 117th in the world. The growth of gross domestic product in Bermuda (3.5%) was less than growth of gross domestic product in the world (4.1%), was less than growth of gross domestic product in the Americas (4.1%).

Comparison with neighbors. The Bermuda's gross domestic product was less than in the USA ($1.7 trillion) and in the Bahamas ($1.1 billion). The Bermuda's gross domestic product per capita was greater than in the USA ($7.8 thousand) and in the Bahamas ($6.1 thousand). The growth of gross domestic product in Bermuda was greater than in the Bahamas (2.4%); but less than in the United States (3.5%).

Comparison with leaders. The Bermuda's gross domestic product was less than in the USA ($1.7 trillion), in the USSR ($649.4 billion), in Japan ($558.0 billion), in Germany ($484.2 billion), and in France ($333.2 billion). The Bermudian GDP per capita was greater than in the USA ($7.8 thousand), in France ($6.2 thousand), in Germany ($6.1 thousand), in Japan ($5.0 thousand), and in the USSR ($2.6 thousand). The growth of gross domestic product in Bermuda was greater than in Germany (3.1%); but less than in the USSR (4.8%), in Japan (4.6%), in France (3.9%), and in the United States (3.5%).

The 1980s

The gross domestic product of Bermuda was $1.4 billion per year in the 1980s, ranked 128th in the world, and was on a par with Monaco ($1.4 billion), Benin ($1.4 billion). The share in the world was 0.0093%, and 0.026% in the Americas.

The gross domestic product of Bermuda included: household consumption expenditure (65.7%), capital formation (19.2%), public expenditure (11.1%), and net export (5.6%).

The Bermuda's GDP per capita was $23 700.1 in the 1980s, ranked 5th in the world. The GDP per capita in Bermuda was greater than gross domestic product per capita in the world ($3 123.4) in 7.6 times, and was greater than GDP per capita in the Americas ($8 168.9) in 2.9 times.

The growth of gross domestic product in Bermuda was 1.3% in the 1980s, ranked 145th in the world. The growth of GDP in Bermuda (1.3%) was less than growth of GDP in the world (3.0%), was less than growth of gross domestic product in the Americas (2.8%).

Comparison with neighbors. The Bermudian gross domestic product was less than in the United States ($4.2 trillion) and in the Bahamas ($3.2 billion). The Bermuda's gross domestic product per capita was greater than in the United States ($17.4 thousand) and in the Bahamas ($14.0 thousand). The growth of GDP in Bermuda was less than in the Bahamas (3.9%) and in the USA (3.1%).

Comparison with leaders. The GDP of Bermuda was less than in the United States ($4.2 trillion), in Japan ($1.8 trillion), in Germany ($990.0 billion), in the USSR ($887.0 billion), and in France ($729.5 billion). The Bermudian gross domestic product per capita was greater than in the United States ($17.4 thousand), in Japan ($15.0 thousand), in France ($12.9 thousand), in Germany ($12.7 thousand), and in the USSR ($3.2 thousand). The growth of GDP in Bermuda was less than in the USSR (4.3%), in Japan (4.3%), in the USA (3.1%), in France (2.3%), and in Germany (1.9%).

The 1990s

The gross domestic product of Bermuda was $2.6 billion per year in the 1990s, ranked 145th in the world, and was on a par with Congo ($2.6 billion). The share in the world was 0.0090%, and 0.026% in the Americas.

The gross domestic product of Bermuda consisted of: household expenditure (64.9%), capital formation (16.2%), government consumption expenditure (11.8%), and net export (6.9%).

The Bermuda's GDP per capita was $40 536.7 in the 1990s, ranked 6th in the world. The gross domestic product per capita in Bermuda was greater than gross domestic product per capita in the world ($5 020.1) in 8.1 times, and was greater than GDP per capita in the Americas ($12 984.7) in 3.1 times.

The growth of GDP in Bermuda was 2% in the 1990s, ranked 138th in the world, and was on a par with the Bahamas (2.0%). The growth of gross domestic product in Bermuda (2.0%) was less than growth of GDP in the world (2.8%), was less than growth of GDP in the Americas (3.1%).

Comparison with neighbors. The GDP of Bermuda was less than in the United States ($7.6 trillion) and in the Bahamas ($5.6 billion). The Bermudian GDP per capita was greater than in the United States ($28.7 thousand) and in the Bahamas ($20.1 thousand). The growth of gross domestic product in Bermuda was greater than in the Bahamas (2.0%); but less than in the United States (3.2%).

Comparison with leaders. The gross domestic product of Bermuda was less than in the United States ($7.6 trillion), in Japan ($4.3 trillion), in Germany ($2.2 trillion), in France ($1.4 trillion), and in the UK ($1.3 trillion). The Bermudian GDP per capita was greater than in Japan ($34.3 thousand), in the USA ($28.7 thousand), in Germany ($27.0 thousand), in France ($24.1 thousand), and in the United Kingdom ($22.9 thousand). The growth of GDP in Bermuda was greater than in Japan (1.5%); but less than in the USA (3.2%), in the United Kingdom (2.3%), in Germany (2.2%), and in France (2.0%).

The 2000s

The Bermuda's gross domestic product was $4.9 billion per year in the 2000s, ranked 143rd in the world. The share in the world was 0.011%, and 0.029% in the Americas.

The GDP of Bermuda included: household consumption expenditure (50.7%), capital formation (16.5%), government expenditure (14.0%), and net export (17.1%).

The Bermuda's GDP per capita was $74 724.2 in the 2000s, ranked 5th in the world. The Bermudian GDP per capita was greater than GDP per capita in the world ($7 176.3) in 10.4 times, and was greater than GDP per capita in the Americas ($19 020.5) in 3.9 times.

The growth of GDP in Bermuda was 2.8% in the 2000s, ranked 144th in the world. The growth of gross domestic product in Bermuda (2.8%) was less than growth of GDP in the world (3.0%), was greater than growth of GDP in the Americas (2.1%).

Comparison with neighbors. The GDP of Bermuda was less than in the USA ($12.6 trillion) and in the Bahamas ($9.4 billion). The gross domestic product per capita in Bermuda was greater than in the United States ($42.8 thousand) and in the Bahamas ($29.2 thousand). The growth of GDP in Bermuda was greater than in the United States (1.9%) and in the Bahamas (0.96%).

Comparison with leaders. The Bermuda's GDP was less than in the USA ($12.6 trillion), in Japan ($4.7 trillion), in Germany ($2.8 trillion), in China ($2.6 trillion), and in the UK ($2.3 trillion). The GDP per capita in Bermuda was greater than in the United States ($42.8 thousand), in the United Kingdom ($38.4 thousand), in Japan ($36.4 thousand), in Germany ($34.0 thousand), and in China ($1 954.1). The growth of GDP in Bermuda was greater than in the United States (1.9%), in the UK (1.7%), in Germany (0.73%), and in Japan (0.50%); but less than in China (10.3%).

The 2010s

The Bermudian GDP was $6.8 billion per year in the 2010s, ranked 153rd in the world, and was on a par with Mauritania ($6.7 billion). The share in the world was 0.0087%, and 0.027% in the Americas.

The gross domestic product of Bermuda consisted of: household expenditure (48.3%), government expenditure (12.8%), capital formation (12.7%), and net export (26.3%).

The Bermuda's GDP per capita was $105 677.4 in the 2010s, ranked 4th in the world. The GDP per capita in Bermuda was greater than gross domestic product per capita in the world ($10 603.1) in 10.0 times, and was greater than gross domestic product per capita in the Americas ($26 129.9) in 4.0 times.

The growth of GDP in Bermuda was -0.7% in the 2010s, ranked 199th in the world. The growth of gross domestic product in Bermuda (-0.66%) was less than growth of gross domestic product in the world (3.1%), was less than growth of gross domestic product in the Americas (2.2%).

Comparison with neighbors. The GDP of Bermuda was 2 659.9 times lower than in the United States ($18.0 trillion) and 41.4% lower than in the Bahamas ($11.5 billion). The gross domestic product per capita in Bermuda was 88.0% higher than in the United States ($56.2 thousand) and 3.4 times higher than in the Bahamas ($31.0 thousand). The growth of gross domestic product in Bermuda was less than in the USA (2.3%) and in the Bahamas (1.3%).

Comparison with leaders. The Bermudian gross domestic product was 2 659.9 times lower than in the United States ($18.0 trillion), 1 555.8 times lower than in China ($10.5 trillion), 774.3 times lower than in Japan ($5.2 trillion), 542.2 times lower than in Germany ($3.7 trillion), and 409.7 times lower than in the United Kingdom ($2.8 trillion). The gross domestic product per capita in Bermuda was 88.0% higher than in the USA ($56.2 thousand), 2.4 times higher than in Germany ($44.7 thousand), 2.5 times higher than in the UK ($42.2 thousand), 2.6 times higher than in Japan ($40.9 thousand), and 14.1 times higher than in China ($7.5 thousand). The growth of gross domestic product in Bermuda was less than in China (7.7%), in the USA (2.3%), in Germany (1.9%), in the UK (1.8%), and in Japan (1.3%).

Chapter II. Value added

The Bermuda's value added grew up from $474.4 million per year in the 1970s to $6.5 billion per year in the 2010s, that is by $6.0 billion or 13.6 times. The change occurred at $5.5 billion due to a 6.8-fold increase in prices, as also at $402.4 million due to a 1.7-fold increase in productivity, as well as at $76.5 million due to the rise in population. The average annual growth in value added is 1.7%. The minimum value of value added was in 1970 at $264.1 million. The maximum value of value added was in 2019 at $7.0 billion.

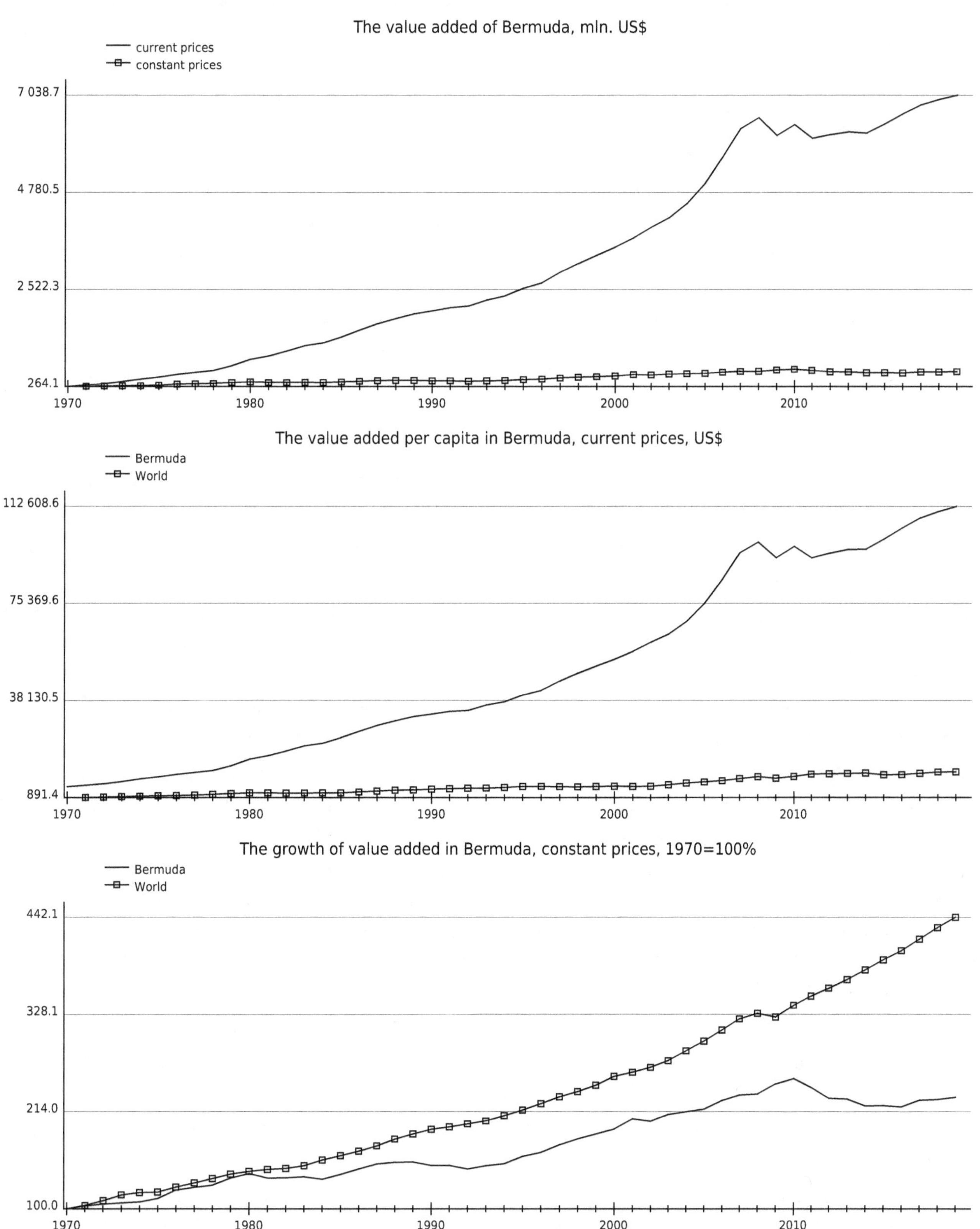

The value added of Bermuda, mln. US$

The value added per capita in Bermuda, current prices, US$

The growth of value added in Bermuda, constant prices, 1970=100%

The 1970s

The value added of Bermuda was $474.4 million per year in the 1970s, ranked 140th in the world, and was on a par with Malta ($476.3 million), Somalia ($485.2 million), Palestine ($486.4 million). The share in the world was 0.0075%, and 0.021% in the Americas.

The total value added of Bermuda included: services (64.0%), trade (17.6%), transportation (7.2%), construction (5.6%), industry (4.8%), and agriculture (0.77%).

The Bermuda's value added per capita was $8 622.2 in the 1970s, ranked 8th in the world. The Bermudian value added per capita was greater than value added per capita in the world ($1 564.4) in 5.5 times, and was greater than value added per capita in the Americas ($3 985.3) in 2.2 times.

The growth of value added in Bermuda was 3.5% in the 1970s, ranked 124th in the world, and was on a par with Europe (3.4%), Mali (3.5%), the Americas (3.5%). The growth of value added in Bermuda (3.5%) was less than growth of value added in the world (3.9%), was less than growth of value added in the Americas (3.5%).

Comparison with neighbors. The value added of Bermuda was less than in the USA ($1.7 trillion) and in the Bahamas ($1.0 billion). The value added per capita in Bermuda was greater than in the United States ($7.8 thousand) and in the Bahamas ($5.5 thousand). The growth of value added in Bermuda was greater than in the United States (2.9%) and in the Bahamas (2.4%).

Comparison with leaders. The value added of Bermuda was less than in the USA ($1.7 trillion), in the USSR ($649.4 billion), in Japan ($545.3 billion), in Germany ($444.9 billion), and in France ($297.3 billion). The value added per capita in Bermuda was greater than in the United States ($7.8 thousand), in Germany ($5.7 thousand), in France ($5.5 thousand), in Japan ($4.9 thousand), and in the USSR ($2.6 thousand). The growth of value added in Bermuda was greater than in Germany (3.1%) and in the USA (2.9%); but less than in Japan (4.9%), in the USSR (4.8%), and in France (3.7%).

The 1980s

The Bermudian value added was $1.4 billion per year in the 1980s, ranked 124th in the world, and was on a par with Barbados ($1.4 billion), Malta ($1.4 billion), Monaco ($1.4 billion). The share in the world was 0.0096%, and 0.026% in the Americas.

The total value added of Bermuda consisted of: services (64.0%), trade (17.6%), transportation (7.2%), construction (5.6%), industry (4.8%), and agriculture (0.77%).

The Bermudian value added per capita was $23 574.3 in the 1980s, ranked 5th in the world. The value added per capita in Bermuda was greater than value added per capita in the world ($3 029.9) in 7.8 times, and was greater than value added per capita in the Americas ($8 159.2) in 2.9 times.

The growth of value added in Bermuda was 1.3% in the 1980s, ranked 148th in the world. The growth of value added in Bermuda (1.3%) was less than growth of value added in the world (2.9%), was less than growth of value added in the Americas (2.7%).

Comparison with neighbors. The value added of Bermuda was less than in the United States ($4.2 trillion) and in the Bahamas ($2.9 billion). The value added per capita in Bermuda was greater than in the USA ($17.4 thousand) and in the Bahamas ($12.6 thousand). The growth of value added in Bermuda was less than in the Bahamas (3.8%) and in the USA (2.8%).

Comparison with leaders. The value added of Bermuda was less than in the USA ($4.2 trillion), in Japan ($1.8 trillion), in Germany ($907.0 billion), in the USSR ($887.0 billion), and in France ($650.9 billion). The value added per capita in Bermuda was greater than in the USA ($17.4 thousand), in Japan ($14.8 thousand), in Germany ($11.6 thousand), in France ($11.5 thousand), and in the USSR ($3.2 thousand). The growth of value added in Bermuda was less than in the USSR (4.3%), in Japan (4.2%), in the USA (2.8%), in France (2.2%), and in Germany (2.0%).

The 1990s

The Bermudian value added was $2.6 billion per year in the 1990s, ranked 144th in the world, and was on a par with Moldova ($2.5 billion). The share in the world was 0.0093%, and 0.026% in the Americas.

The total value added of Bermuda included: services (64.1%), trade (17.6%), transportation (7.2%), construction (5.6%), industry (4.7%), and agriculture (0.77%).

The Bermudian value added per capita was $40 351.6 in the 1990s, ranked 6th in the world, and was on a par with San Marino ($40.4 thousand), Luxembourg ($39.9 thousand). The Bermuda's value added per capita was greater than value added per capita in the world

($4 799.9) in 8.4 times, and was greater than value added per capita in the Americas ($12 777.9) in 3.2 times.

The growth of value added in Bermuda was 2% in the 1990s, ranked 135th in the world, and was on a par with Greece (1.9%), the FSM (1.9%), Venezuela (2.0%). The growth of value added in Bermuda (2.0%) was less than growth of value added in the world (2.7%), was less than growth of value added in the Americas (2.8%).

Comparison with neighbors. The value added of Bermuda was less than in the United States ($7.6 trillion) and in the Bahamas ($5.2 billion). The value added per capita in Bermuda was greater than in the USA ($28.6 thousand) and in the Bahamas ($18.9 thousand). The growth of value added in Bermuda was greater than in the Bahamas (1.9%); but less than in the United States (2.8%).

Comparison with leaders. The Bermuda's value added was less than in the USA ($7.6 trillion), in Japan ($4.3 trillion), in Germany ($2.0 trillion), in France ($1.3 trillion), and in the United Kingdom ($1.2 trillion). The Bermuda's value added per capita was greater than in Japan ($34.2 thousand), in the USA ($28.6 thousand), in Germany ($24.5 thousand), in France ($21.6 thousand), and in the UK ($21.4 thousand). The growth of value added in Bermuda was greater than in France (1.8%) and in Japan (1.8%); but less than in the USA (2.8%), in the United Kingdom (2.4%), and in Germany (2.1%).

The 2000s

The value added of Bermuda was $4.9 billion per year in the 2000s, ranked 140th in the world, and was on a par with Guinea ($4.8 billion), French Polynesia ($4.8 billion). The share in the world was 0.011%, and 0.030% in the Americas.

The total value added of Bermuda included: services (71.2%), trade (12.9%), transportation (6.1%), construction (5.8%), industry (3.4%), and agriculture (0.67%).

The Bermudian value added per capita was $75 030.2 in the 2000s, ranked 3rd in the world, and was on a par with the Cayman Islands ($73.6 thousand). The value added per capita in Bermuda was greater than value added per capita in the world ($6 818.0) in 11.0 times, and was greater than value added per capita in the Americas ($18 623.4) in 4.0 times.

The growth of value added in Bermuda was 2.8% in the 2000s, ranked 138th in the world. The growth of value added in Bermuda (2.8%) was less than growth of value added in the world (2.9%), was greater than growth of value added in the Americas (1.9%).

Comparison with neighbors. The value added of Bermuda was less than in the USA ($12.6 trillion) and in the Bahamas ($8.8 billion). The value added per capita in Bermuda was greater than in the United States ($42.8 thousand) and in the Bahamas ($27.2 thousand). The growth of value added in Bermuda was greater than in the United States (1.7%) and in the Bahamas (0.73%).

Comparison with leaders. The value added of Bermuda was less than in the United States ($12.6 trillion), in Japan ($4.7 trillion), in China ($2.6 trillion), in Germany ($2.5 trillion), and in the UK ($2.1 trillion). The value added per capita in Bermuda was greater than in the United States ($42.8 thousand), in Japan ($36.4 thousand), in the UK ($34.6 thousand), in Germany ($30.7 thousand), and in China ($1 954.1). The growth of value added in Bermuda was greater than in the USA (1.7%), in the United Kingdom (1.7%), in Germany (0.65%), and in Japan (0.27%); but less than in China (10.2%).

The 2010s

The value added of Bermuda was $6.5 billion per year in the 2010s, ranked 151st in the world, and was on a par with Monaco ($6.5 billion), Kyrgyzstan ($6.3 billion). The share in the world was 0.0087%, and 0.026% in the Americas.

The total value added of Bermuda consisted of: services (78.7%), trade (10.1%), transportation (5.1%), construction (3.6%), industry (2.2%), and agriculture (0.29%).

The Bermuda's value added per capita was $101 187.9 in the 2010s, ranked 3rd in the world, and was on a par with Luxembourg ($99.9 thousand). The Bermudian value added per capita was greater than value added per capita in the world ($10 094.6) in 10.0 times, and was greater than value added per capita in the Americas ($25 411.8) in 4.0 times.

The growth of value added in Bermuda was -0.7% in the 2010s, ranked 198th in the world. The growth of value added in Bermuda (-0.66%) was less than growth of value added in the world (3.1%), was less than growth of value added in the Americas (2.1%).

Comparison with neighbors. The Bermudian value added was 2 777.9 times lower than in the USA ($18.0 trillion) and 37.7% lower than in the Bahamas ($10.4 billion). The value added per capita in Bermuda was 80.0% higher than in the USA ($56.2 thousand) and 3.6 times higher than in the Bahamas ($27.9 thousand). The growth of value added in Bermuda was less than in the USA (2.2%) and in the Bahamas (1.6%).

Comparison with leaders. The value added of Bermuda was 2 777.9 times lower than in the United States ($18.0 trillion), 1 624.9 times lower than in China ($10.5 trillion), 804.5 times lower than in Japan ($5.2 trillion), 510.8 times lower than in Germany ($3.3 trillion), and 382.1 times lower than in the United Kingdom ($2.5 trillion). The Bermuda's value added per capita was 80.0% higher than in the USA ($56.2 thousand), 2.5 times higher than in Japan ($40.7 thousand), 2.5 times higher than in Germany ($40.3 thousand), 2.7 times higher than in the UK ($37.7 thousand), and 13.5 times higher than in China ($7.5 thousand). The growth of value added in Bermuda was less than in China (7.7%), in the United States (2.2%), in Germany (1.9%), in the United Kingdom (1.8%), and in Japan (1.3%).

Chapter III. Gross national income

The GNI of Bermuda grew from $506.4 million per year in the 1970s to $6.8 billion per year in the 2010s, that is by $6.3 billion or 13.5 times. The change occurred at $5.9 billion due to a 7.1-fold increase in prices, as also at $374.7 million due to a 1.6-fold increase in productivity, as well as at $81.7 million due to the increase in population. The average annual growth in gross national income is 1.6%. The minimum value of GNI was in 1970 at $282.8 million. The maximum value of GNI was in 2019 at $7.4 billion.

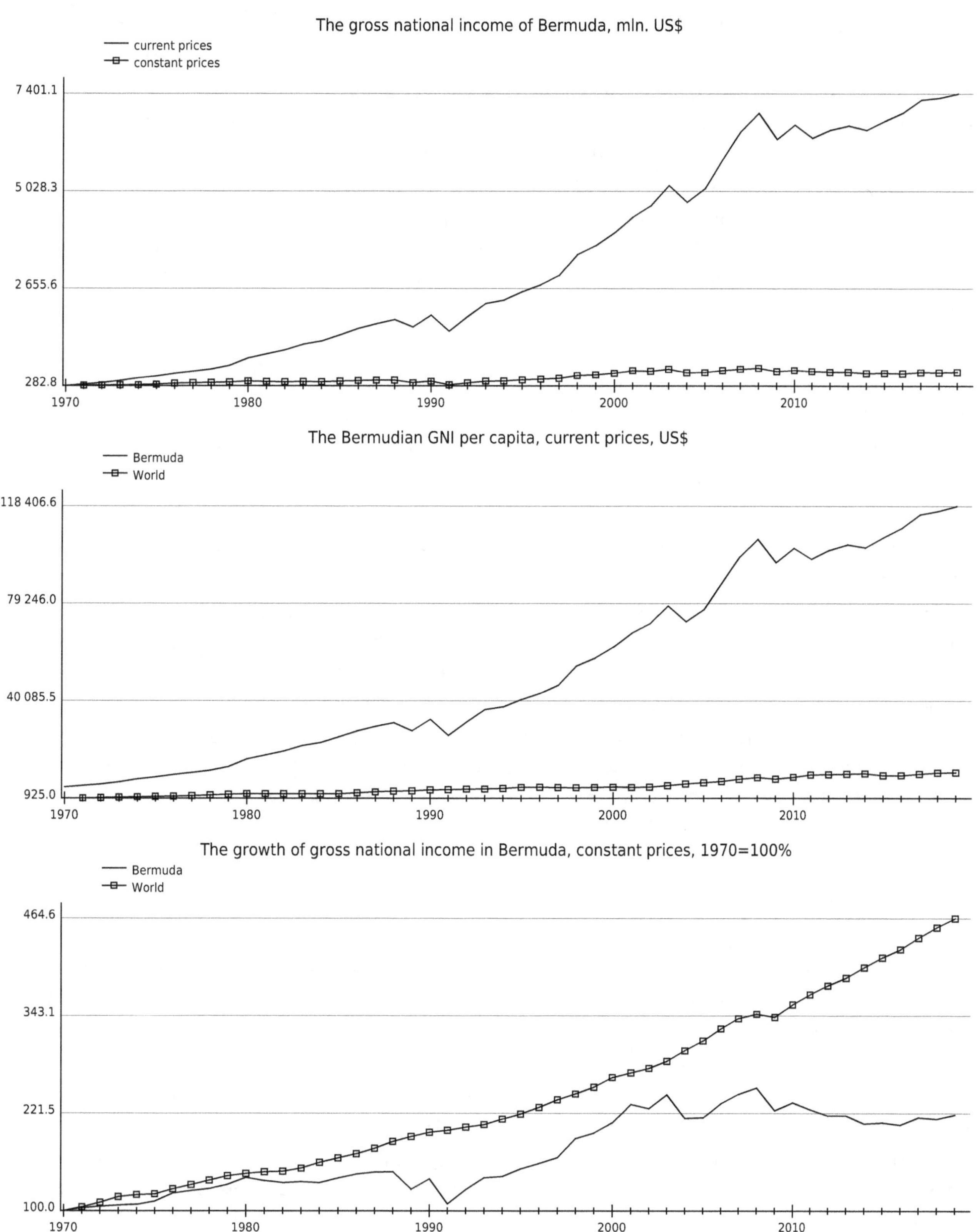

The 1970s

The Bermudian GNI was $506.4 million per year in the 1970s, ranked 137th in the world, and was on a par with Somalia ($503.1 million). The share in the world was 0.0077%, and 0.023% in the Americas.

The Bermudian gross national income per capita was $9 203.0 in the 1970s, ranked 7th in the world, and was on a par with Sweden ($9.0 thousand). The GNI per capita in Bermuda was greater than gross national income per capita in the world ($1 624.3) in 5.7 times, and was greater than GNI per capita in the Americas ($4 019.9) in 2.3 times.

The growth of GNI in Bermuda was 3.2% in the 1970s, ranked 128th in the world, and was on a par with the Virgin Islands (3.2%). The growth of GNI in Bermuda (3.2%) was less than growth of GNI in the world (4.1%), was less than growth of GNI in the Americas (4.0%).

Comparison with neighbors. The gross national income of Bermuda was less than in the United States ($1.7 trillion) and in the Bahamas ($1.1 billion). The gross national income per capita in Bermuda was greater than in the United States ($7.8 thousand) and in the Bahamas ($5.8 thousand). The growth of GNI in Bermuda was less than in the Bahamas (4.2%) and in the USA (3.5%).

Comparison with leaders. The gross national income of Bermuda was less than in the USA ($1.7 trillion), in the USSR ($649.4 billion), in Japan ($558.5 billion), in Germany ($486.2 billion), and in France ($334.3 billion). The GNI per capita in Bermuda was greater than in the USA ($7.8 thousand), in France ($6.2 thousand), in Germany ($6.2 thousand), in Japan ($5.0 thousand), and in the USSR ($2.6 thousand). The growth of GNI in Bermuda was greater than in Germany (3.0%); but less than in the USSR (4.8%), in Japan (4.7%), in France (3.9%), and in the USA (3.5%).

The 1980s

The GNI of Bermuda was $1.4 billion per year in the 1980s, ranked 127th in the world, and was on a par with Mauritius ($1.5 billion), Barbados ($1.4 billion), Suriname ($1.4 billion). The share in the world was 0.0096%, and 0.027% in the Americas.

The Bermuda's GNI per capita was $24 376.6 in the 1980s, ranked 5th in the world. The Bermudian gross national income per capita was greater than GNI per capita in the world ($3 117.1) in 7.8 times, and was greater than gross national income per capita in the Americas ($8 063.2) in 3.0 times.

The growth of gross national income in Bermuda was -0.5% in the 1980s, ranked 164th in the world. The growth of GNI in Bermuda (-0.47%) was less than growth of gross national income in the world (3.0%), was less than growth of GNI in the Americas (2.8%).

Comparison with neighbors. The GNI of Bermuda was less than in the United States ($4.2 trillion) and in the Bahamas ($2.8 billion). The gross national income per capita in Bermuda was greater than in the United States ($17.4 thousand) and in the Bahamas ($12.2 thousand). The growth of gross national income in Bermuda was less than in the Bahamas (3.4%) and in the USA (3.1%).

Comparison with leaders. The Bermudian gross national income was less than in the United States ($4.2 trillion), in Japan ($1.8 trillion), in Germany ($996.5 billion), in the USSR ($887.0 billion), and in France ($732.1 billion). The gross national income per capita in Bermuda was greater than in the USA ($17.4 thousand), in Japan ($15.0 thousand), in France ($13.0 thousand), in Germany ($12.8 thousand), and in the USSR ($3.2 thousand). The growth of GNI in Bermuda was less than in Japan (4.4%), in the USSR (4.3%), in the United States (3.1%), in France (2.3%), and in Germany (2.0%).

The 1990s

The gross national income of Bermuda was $2.6 billion per year in the 1990s, ranked 144th in the world. The share in the world was 0.0091%, and 0.026% in the Americas.

The Bermudian GNI per capita was $40 730.7 in the 1990s, ranked 6th in the world. The Bermudian gross national income per capita was greater than gross national income per capita in the world ($4 991.4) in 8.2 times, and was greater than GNI per capita in the Americas ($12 792.4) in 3.2 times.

The growth of gross national income in Bermuda was 4.5% in the 1990s, ranked 58th in the world, and was on a par with Namibia (4.5%), Belize (4.5%), Tuvalu (4.5%). The growth of GNI in Bermuda (4.5%) was greater than growth of gross national income in the world (2.8%), was greater than growth of gross national income in the Americas (3.2%).

Comparison with neighbors. The Bermudian GNI was less than in the United States ($7.5 trillion) and in the Bahamas ($5.5 billion). The Bermuda's GNI per capita was greater than in the United States ($28.5 thousand) and in the Bahamas ($19.9 thousand). The growth of GNI in Bermuda was greater than in the United States (3.4%) and in the Bahamas (2.3%).

Comparison with leaders. The Bermudian GNI was less than in the United States ($7.5 trillion), in Japan ($4.4 trillion), in Germany ($2.2 trillion), in France ($1.4 trillion), and in the United Kingdom ($1.3 trillion). The gross national income per capita in Bermuda was greater than in Japan ($34.7 thousand), in the USA ($28.5 thousand), in Germany ($27.0 thousand), in France ($24.3 thousand), and in the UK ($23.0 thousand). The growth of gross national income in Bermuda was greater than in the United States (3.4%), in France (2.2%), in the UK (2.0%), in Germany (2.0%), and in Japan (1.5%).

The 2000s

The Bermudian GNI was $5.4 billion per year in the 2000s, ranked 140th in the world, and was on a par with Chad ($5.3 billion), French Polynesia ($5.4 billion). The share in the world was 0.012%, and 0.032% in the Americas.

The GNI per capita in Bermuda was $81 412.0 in the 2000s, ranked 3rd in the world. The gross national income per capita in Bermuda was greater than GNI per capita in the world ($7 165.2) in 11.4 times, and was greater than gross national income per capita in the Americas ($18 970.5) in 4.3 times.

The growth of GNI in Bermuda was 1.3% in the 2000s, ranked 181st in the world. The growth of gross national income in Bermuda (1.3%) was less than growth of gross national income in the world (3.0%), was less than growth of gross national income in the Americas (2.1%).

Comparison with neighbors. The GNI of Bermuda was less than in the USA ($12.7 trillion) and in the Bahamas ($9.5 billion). The gross national income per capita in Bermuda was greater than in the United States ($43.2 thousand) and in the Bahamas ($29.5 thousand). The growth of GNI in Bermuda was greater than in the Bahamas (0.93%); but less than in the United States (1.8%).

Comparison with leaders. The GNI of Bermuda was less than in the USA ($12.7 trillion), in Japan ($4.8 trillion), in Germany ($2.8 trillion), in China ($2.6 trillion), and in the UK ($2.3 trillion). The GNI per capita in Bermuda was greater than in the United States ($43.2 thousand), in the United Kingdom ($38.5 thousand), in Japan ($37.1 thousand), in Germany ($34.2 thousand), and in China ($1 950.5). The growth of gross national income in Bermuda was greater than in Germany (1.0%) and in Japan (0.62%); but less than in China (10.4%), in the USA (1.8%), and in the United Kingdom (1.7%).

The 2010s

The GNI of Bermuda was $6.8 billion per year in the 2010s, ranked 152nd in the world. The share in the world was 0.0088%, and 0.027% in the Americas.

The gross national income per capita in Bermuda was $106 824.1 in the 2010s, ranked 3rd in the world. The GNI per capita in Bermuda was greater than GNI per capita in the world ($10 611.7) in 10.1 times, and was greater than gross national income per capita in the Americas ($26 262.7) in 4.1 times.

The growth of GNI in Bermuda was -0.2% in the 2010s, ranked 197th in the world. The growth of gross national income in Bermuda (-0.24%) was less than growth of GNI in the world (3.1%), was less than growth of gross national income in the Americas (2.3%).

Comparison with neighbors. The Bermudian gross national income was 2 681.9 times lower than in the USA ($18.3 trillion) and 38.0% lower than in the Bahamas ($11.0 billion). The GNI per capita in Bermuda was 86.4% higher than in the USA ($57.3 thousand) and 3.6 times higher than in the Bahamas ($29.6 thousand). The growth of GNI in Bermuda was less than in the United States (2.5%) and in the Bahamas (0.13%).

Comparison with leaders. The gross national income of Bermuda was 2 681.9 times lower than in the USA ($18.3 trillion), 1 533.5 times lower than in China ($10.5 trillion), 791.0 times lower than in Japan ($5.4 trillion), 549.2 times lower than in Germany ($3.7 trillion), and 402.3 times lower than in France ($2.7 trillion). The Bermuda's gross national income per capita was 86.4% higher than in the USA ($57.3 thousand), 2.3 times higher than in Germany ($45.8 thousand), 2.5 times higher than in Japan ($42.2 thousand), 2.6 times higher than in France ($41.4 thousand), and 14.3 times higher than in China ($7.5 thousand). The growth of GNI in Bermuda was less than in China (7.7%), in the USA (2.5%), in Germany (2.0%), in Japan (1.4%), and in France (1.4%).

Part II. Structure

The 2010s
agriculture   0.29%
industry   2.2%
construction   3.6%
trade   10.1%
transportation   5.1%
services   78.7%

Chapter IV. Agriculture

Agriculture, hunting, forestry, fishing (ISIC A-B)

The agriculture of Bermuda grew up from $3.7 million per year in the 1970s to $18.7 million per year in the 2010s, that is by $15.0 million or 5.1 times. The change occurred at $14.8 million due to a 4.8-fold increase in prices, as also at -$371.1 thousand due to a 1.1-fold decrease in productivity, as well as at $592.1 thousand due to the expansion in population. The average annual growth in agriculture is 0.46%. The minimum value of agriculture was in 1970 at $2.0 million. The maximum value of agriculture was in 2006 at $46.4 million.

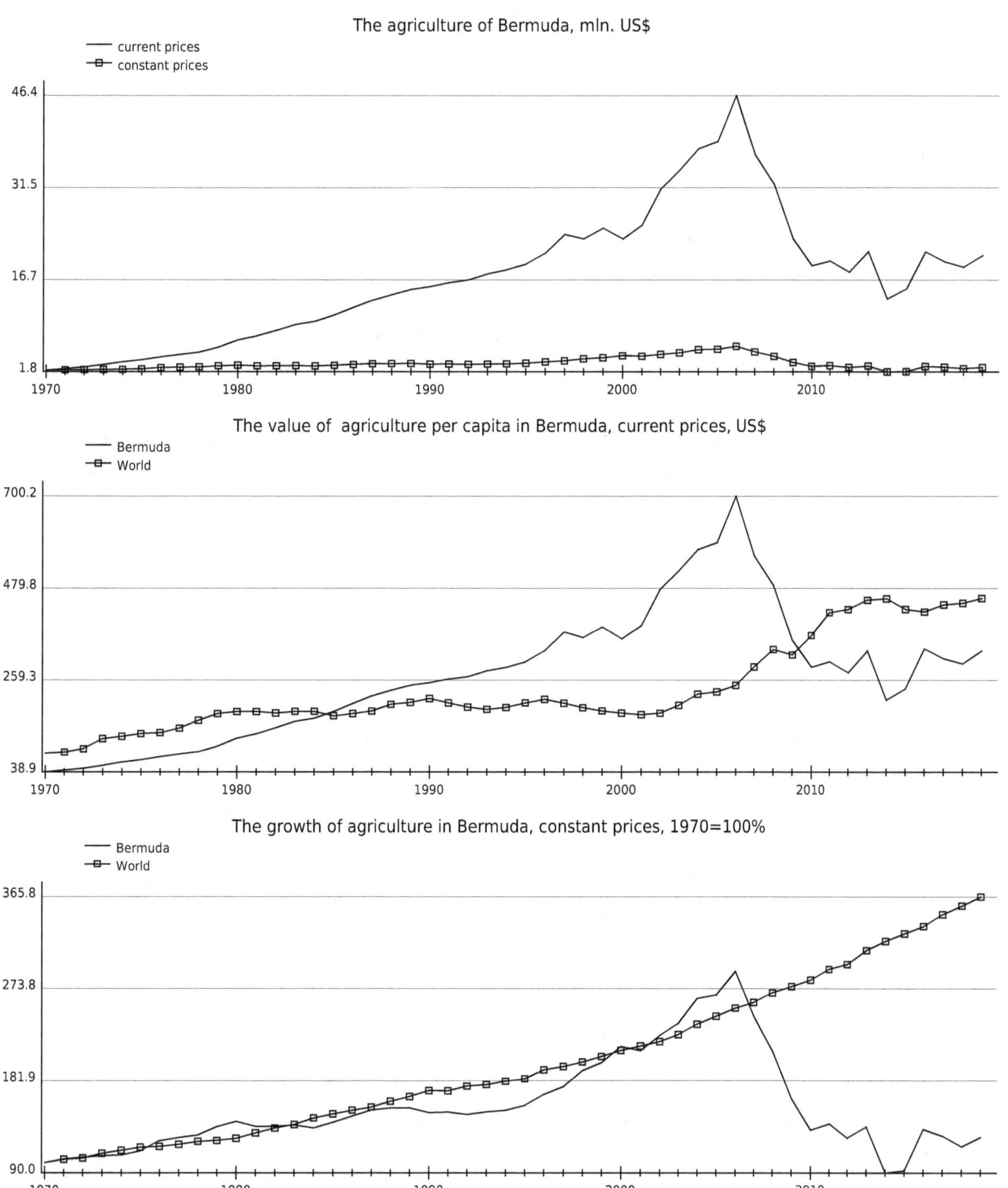

The agriculture of Bermuda, mln. US$

The value of agriculture per capita in Bermuda, current prices, US$

The growth of agriculture in Bermuda, constant prices, 1970=100%

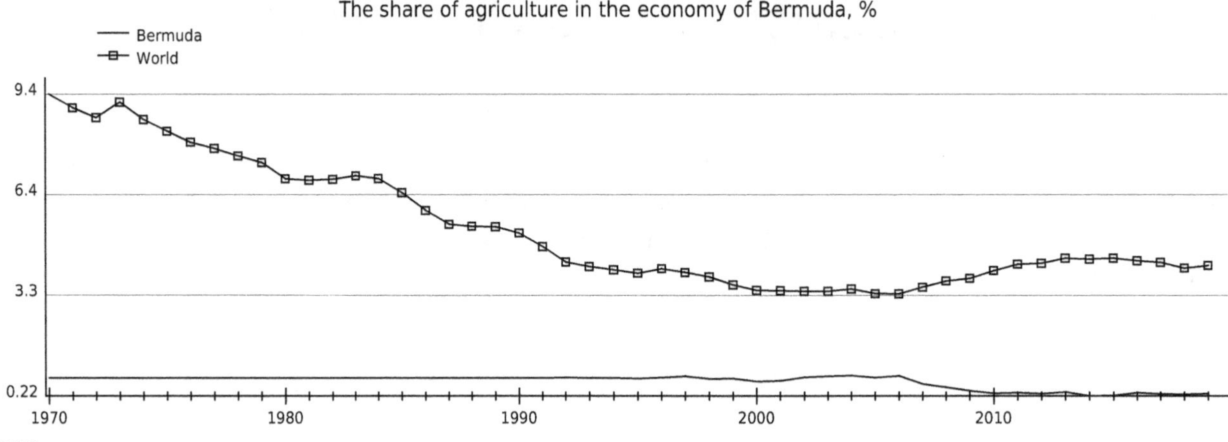

The 1970s

The value of agriculture in Bermuda was $3.7 million per year in the 1970s, ranked 169th in the world. The share in the world was 0.0007%, and 0.0041% in the Americas.

The share of agriculture in the economy of Bermuda was 0.77% in the 1970s, ranked 175th in the world.

The Bermuda's agriculture per capita was $66.7 in the 1970s, ranked 138th in the world, and was on a par with Somalia ($66.3), Haiti ($66.3), Nepal ($67.4). The sector of agriculture per capita in Bermuda was less than agriculture per capita in the world ($127.6) by 47.7%, and was less than agriculture per capita in the Americas ($158.1) in 2.4 times.

The growth of agriculture in Bermuda was 3.5% in the 1970s, ranked 77th in the world, and was on a par with Israel (3.5%). The growth of agriculture in Bermuda (3.5%) was greater than growth of agriculture in the world (2.2%), was greater than growth of agriculture in the Americas (1.9%).

Comparison with neighbors. The sector of agriculture in Bermuda was less than in the United States ($42.6 billion) and in the Bahamas ($23.0 million). The sector of agriculture per capita in Bermuda was less than in the USA ($195.0) and in the Bahamas ($122.6). The growth of agriculture in Bermuda was greater than in the Bahamas (2.4%) and in the United States (0.34%).

Comparison with leaders. The value added of agriculture in Bermuda was less than in the USSR ($88.7 billion), in China ($49.5 billion), in the USA ($42.6 billion), in India ($36.0 billion), and in Japan ($25.8 billion). The value of agriculture per capita in Bermuda was greater than in India ($58.3) and in China ($54.2); but less than in the USSR ($351.8), in Japan ($231.3), and in the USA ($195.0). The growth of agriculture in Bermuda was greater than in China (2.4%), in Japan (0.52%), in the USA (0.34%), and in India (0.30%); but less than in the USSR (7.0%).

The 1980s

The agriculture of Bermuda was $10.8 million per year in the 1980s, ranked 168th in the world. The share in the world was 0.0012%, and 0.0069% in the Americas.

The share of agriculture in the economy of Bermuda was 0.77% in the 1980s, ranked 175th in the world.

The sector of agriculture per capita in Bermuda was $182.4 in the 1980s, ranked 85th in the world, and was on a par with the Seychelles ($179.4), the World ($186.6). The Bermuda's agriculture per capita was less than agriculture per capita in the world ($186.6) by 2.2%, and was less than agriculture per capita in the Americas ($237.6) by 23.2%.

The growth of agriculture in Bermuda was 1.3% in the 1980s, ranked 126th in the world. The growth of agriculture in Bermuda (1.3%) was less than growth of agriculture in the world (3.1%), was less than growth of agriculture in the Americas (2.6%).

Comparison with neighbors. The agriculture of Bermuda was less than in the United States ($68.7 billion) and in the Bahamas ($58.7 million). The Bermuda's agriculture per capita was less than in the USA ($286.8) and in the Bahamas ($253.1). The growth of agriculture in Bermuda was less than in the USA (3.7%) and in the Bahamas (2.9%).

Comparison with leaders. The sector of agriculture in Bermuda was less than in the USSR ($125.8 billion), in China ($94.9 billion), in India ($70.4 billion), in the United States ($68.7 billion), and in Japan ($49.7 billion). The sector of agriculture per capita in Bermuda was greater than in India ($90.7) and in China ($88.5); but less than in the USSR ($457.2), in Japan ($410.0), and in the USA

($286.8). The growth of agriculture in Bermuda was greater than in Japan (0.41%); but less than in China (5.3%), in India (4.4%), in the United States (3.7%), and in the USSR (2.8%).

The 1990s

The sector of agriculture in Bermuda was $19.7 million per year in the 1990s, ranked 189th in the world. The share in the world was 0.0017%, and 0.0088% in the Americas.

The share of agriculture in the economy of Bermuda was 0.77% in the 1990s, ranked 197th in the world, and was on a par with Bahrain (0.77%).

The value added of agriculture per capita in Bermuda was $311.5 in the 1990s, ranked 56th in the world, and was on a par with the Comoros ($305.3). The value added of agriculture per capita in Bermuda was greater than agriculture per capita in the world ($199.8) by 55.9%, and was greater than agriculture per capita in the Americas ($288.9) by 7.8%.

The growth of agriculture in Bermuda was 2.6% in the 1990s, ranked 82nd in the world, and was on a par with the Netherlands (2.6%), Thailand (2.6%), the United States (2.6%). The growth of agriculture in Bermuda (2.6%) was greater than growth of agriculture in the world (2.2%), was greater than growth of agriculture in the Americas (2.4%).

Comparison with neighbors. The value of agriculture in Bermuda was less than in the United States ($96.1 billion) and in the Bahamas ($88.6 million). The agriculture per capita in Bermuda was less than in the United States ($363.4) and in the Bahamas ($320.2). The growth of agriculture in Bermuda was greater than in the Bahamas (0.59%); but less than in the USA (2.6%).

Comparison with leaders. The agriculture of Bermuda was less than in China ($139.0 billion), in the United States ($96.1 billion), in India ($91.4 billion), in Japan ($78.9 billion), and in Brazil ($36.8 billion). The value added of agriculture per capita in Bermuda was greater than in Brazil ($228.7), in China ($112.7), and in India ($95.6); but less than in Japan ($625.5) and in the USA ($363.4). The growth of agriculture in Bermuda was greater than in Japan (-1.8%); but less than in China (4.3%), in Brazil (3.0%), in India (2.8%), and in the United States (2.6%).

The 2000s

The Bermudian agriculture was $33.0 million per year in the 2000s, ranked 184th in the world. The share in the world was 0.0021%, and 0.011% in the Americas.

The share of agriculture in the economy of Bermuda was 0.67% in the 2000s, ranked 193rd in the world.

The value added of agriculture per capita in Bermuda was $501.3 in the 2000s, ranked 26th in the world, and was on a par with Belize ($499.5), Uruguay ($503.6), Suriname ($513.6). The value added of agriculture per capita in Bermuda was greater than agriculture per capita in the world ($240.3) in 2.1 times, and was greater than agriculture per capita in the Americas ($327.5) by 53.1%.

The growth of agriculture in Bermuda was -2% in the 2000s, ranked 182nd in the world. The growth of agriculture in Bermuda (-2.0%) was less than growth of agriculture in the world (3.0%), was less than growth of agriculture in the Americas (2.7%).

Comparison with neighbors. The sector of agriculture in Bermuda was less than in the USA ($122.5 billion) and in the Bahamas ($110.8 million). The value added of agriculture per capita in Bermuda was greater than in the United States ($416.9) and in the Bahamas ($343.3). The growth of agriculture in Bermuda was less than in the USA (3.6%) and in the Bahamas (0.58%).

Comparison with leaders. The value of agriculture in Bermuda was less than in China ($297.7 billion), in India ($147.6 billion), in the United States ($122.5 billion), in Japan ($57.1 billion), and in Nigeria ($47.6 billion). The value added of agriculture per capita in Bermuda was greater than in Japan ($445.6), in the USA ($416.9), in Nigeria ($346.4), in China ($224.5), and in India ($129.7). The growth of agriculture in Bermuda was less than in Nigeria (10.1%), in China (4.0%), in the USA (3.6%), in India (2.0%), and in Japan (-1.3%).

The 2010s

The agriculture of Bermuda was $18.7 million per year in the 2010s, ranked 193rd in the world. The share in the world was 0.0006%, and 0.0038% in the Americas.

The share of agriculture in the economy of Bermuda was 0.29% in the 2010s, ranked 200th in the world.

The value of agriculture per capita in Bermuda was $292.2 in the 2010s, ranked 128th in the world, and was on a par with the Cayman Islands ($292.1), the Philippines ($292.5), Sri Lanka ($290.7). The agriculture per capita in Bermuda was less than agriculture per capita in the world ($432.1) by 32.4%, and was less than agriculture per capita in the Americas ($498.8) by 41.4%.

The growth of agriculture in Bermuda was -2.7% in the 2010s, ranked 193rd in the world. The growth of agriculture in Bermuda (-2.7%) was less than growth of agriculture in the world (2.9%), was less than growth of agriculture in the Americas (2.2%).

Comparison with neighbors. The Bermuda's agriculture was 9 657.0 times lower than in the USA ($180.3 billion) and 5.3 times lower than in the Bahamas ($99.3 million). The value of agriculture per capita in Bermuda was 9.7% higher than in the Bahamas ($266.5); but 48.2% lower than in the USA ($564.3). The growth of agriculture in Bermuda was greater than in the Bahamas (-5.3%); but less than in the USA (2.0%).

Comparison with leaders. The agriculture of Bermuda was 47 469.5 times lower than in China ($886.2 billion), 19 465.7 times lower than in India ($363.4 billion), 9 657.0 times lower than in the USA ($180.3 billion), 6 644.6 times lower than in Indonesia ($124.1 billion), and 5 129.6 times lower than in Nigeria ($95.8 billion). The agriculture per capita in Bermuda was 4.7% higher than in India ($279.1); but 2.2 times lower than in China ($631.9), 48.2% lower than in the USA ($564.3), 45.3% lower than in Nigeria ($534.6), and 39.6% lower than in Indonesia ($483.6). The growth of agriculture in Bermuda was less than in India (4.1%), in Indonesia (3.9%), in China (3.8%), in Nigeria (3.6%), and in the United States (2.0%).

Chapter V. Industry

Mining, Manufacturing, Utilities (ISIC C-E)

The Bermudian industry increased from $22.6 million per year in the 1970s to $140.7 million per year in the 2010s, that is by $118.1 million or 6.2 times. The change occurred at $117.9 million due to a 6.2-fold increase in prices, as also at -$3.5 million due to a 1.2-fold decrease in productivity, as well as at $3.6 million due to the increase in population. The average annual growth in industry is -0.11%. The minimum value of industry was in 1970 at $12.6 million. The maximum value of industry was in 2006 at $179.9 million.

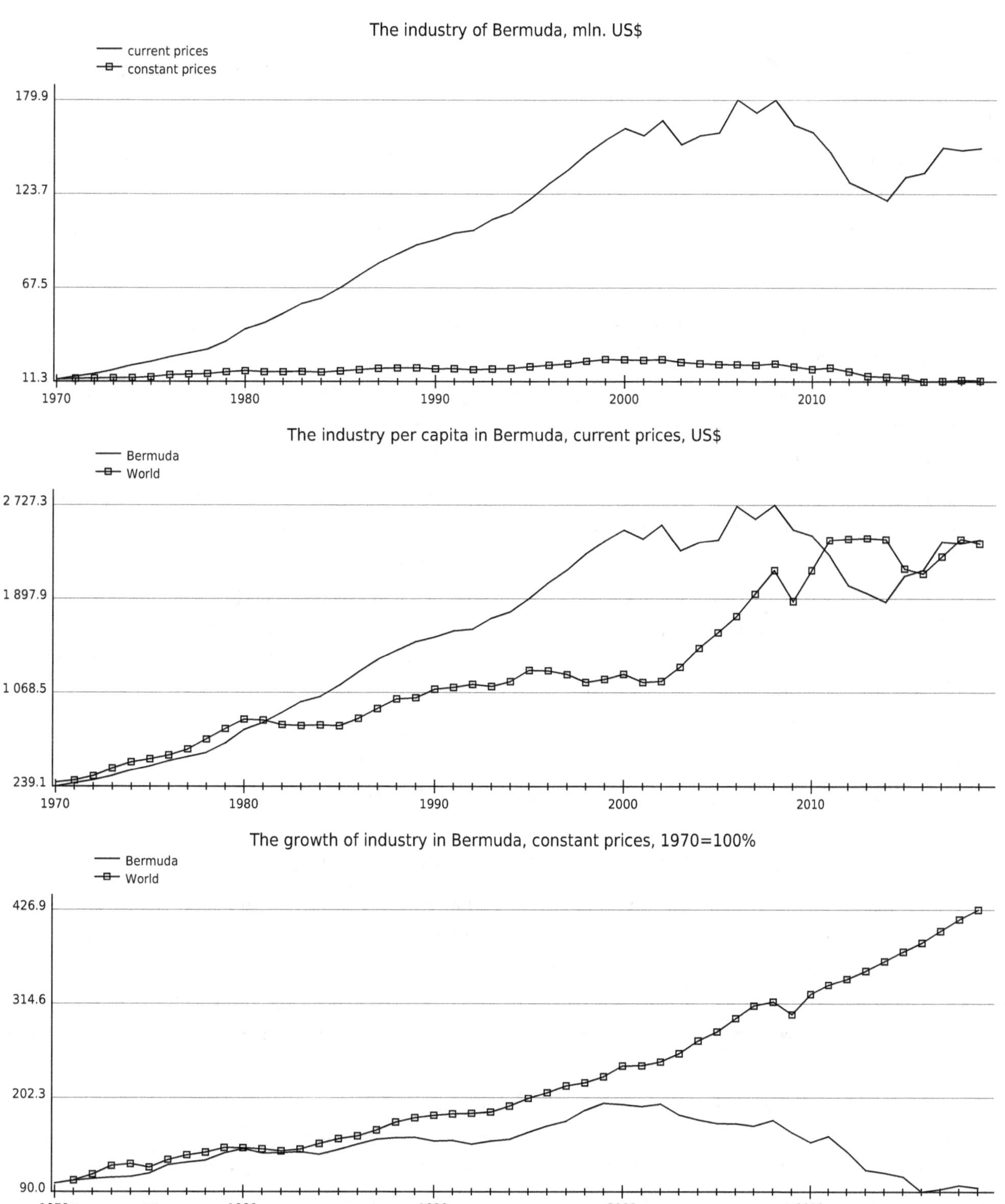

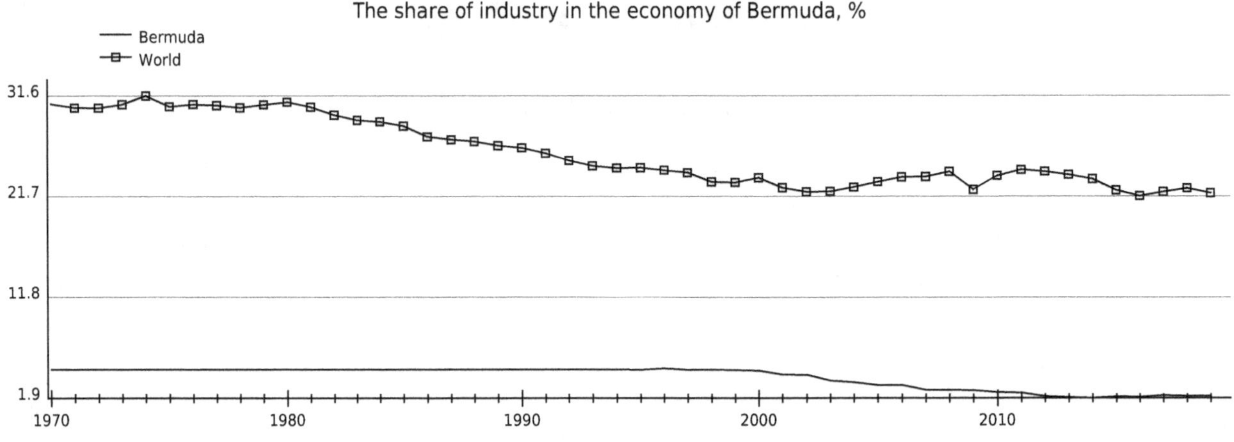

The 1970s

The sector of industry in Bermuda was $22.6 million per year in the 1970s, ranked 151st in the world. The share in the world was 0.0012%, and 0.0037% in the Americas.

The share of industry in the economy of Bermuda was 4.8% in the 1970s, ranked 176th in the world, and was on a par with the Maldives (4.8%).

The Bermudian industry per capita was $410.3 in the 1970s, ranked 59th in the world, and was on a par with Nigeria ($407.3), Iraq ($404.7). The sector of industry per capita in Bermuda was less than industry per capita in the world ($480.5) by 14.6%, and was less than industry per capita in the Americas ($1 091.1) in 2.7 times.

The growth of industry in Bermuda was 3.5% in the 1970s, ranked 122nd in the world, and was on a par with Uruguay (3.4%), Ethiopia (3.5%), Micronesia (3.5%). The growth of industry in Bermuda (3.5%) was less than growth of industry in the world (4.0%), was greater than growth of industry in the Americas (3.2%).

Comparison with neighbors. The Bermudian industry was less than in the United States ($450.4 billion) and in the Bahamas ($74.6 million). The sector of industry per capita in Bermuda was greater than in the Bahamas ($398.2); but less than in the United States ($2.1 thousand). The growth of industry in Bermuda was greater than in the Bahamas (2.4%) and in the United States (2.4%).

Comparison with leaders. The sector of industry in Bermuda was less than in the United States ($450.4 billion), in the USSR ($248.8 billion), in Japan ($185.6 billion), in Germany ($158.4 billion), and in the UK ($72.6 billion). The industry per capita in Bermuda was less than in the USA ($2.1 thousand), in Germany ($2.0 thousand), in Japan ($1 666.5), in the UK ($1 295.1), and in the USSR ($986.6). The growth of industry in Bermuda was greater than in the United States (2.4%), in Germany (2.1%), and in the UK (1.9%); but less than in the USSR (5.2%) and in Japan (4.5%).

The 1980s

The Bermudian industry was $66.6 million per year in the 1980s, ranked 147th in the world. The share in the world was 0.0016%, and 0.0048% in the Americas.

The share of industry in the economy of Bermuda was 4.8% in the 1980s, ranked 178th in the world.

The industry per capita in Bermuda was $1 121.7 in the 1980s, ranked 46th in the world, and was on a par with Mexico ($1 123.6), the USSR ($1 110.8), Czechoslovakia ($1 098.9). The industry per capita in Bermuda was greater than industry per capita in the world ($861.8) by 30.1%, and was less than industry per capita in the Americas ($2 085.6) by 46.2%.

The growth of industry in Bermuda was 1.3% in the 1980s, ranked 131st in the world, and was on a par with France (1.3%). The growth of industry in Bermuda (1.3%) was less than growth of industry in the world (2.3%), was less than growth of industry in the Americas (1.9%).

Comparison with neighbors. The value of industry in Bermuda was less than in the United States ($1.0 trillion) and in the Bahamas ($205.8 million). The Bermuda's industry per capita was greater than in the Bahamas ($888.0); but less than in the United States ($4.2 thousand). The growth of industry in Bermuda was less than in the Bahamas (3.7%) and in the United States (1.9%).

Comparison with leaders. The value added of industry in Bermuda was less than in the United States ($1.0 trillion), in Japan ($566.4

billion), in the USSR ($305.7 billion), in Germany ($297.5 billion), and in the United Kingdom ($171.2 billion). The value added of industry per capita in Bermuda was greater than in the USSR ($1 110.8); but less than in Japan ($4.7 thousand), in the United States ($4.2 thousand), in Germany ($3.8 thousand), and in the United Kingdom ($3.0 thousand). The growth of industry in Bermuda was greater than in Germany (1.2%); but less than in the USSR (5.3%), in Japan (4.2%), in the USA (1.9%), and in the UK (1.4%).

The 1990s

The Bermuda's industry was $121.1 million per year in the 1990s, ranked 169th in the world, and was on a par with Greenland ($121.3 million). The share in the world was 0.0018%, and 0.0058% in the Americas.

The share of industry in the economy of Bermuda was 4.7% in the 1990s, ranked 201st in the world.

The industry per capita in Bermuda was $1 916.0 in the 1990s, ranked 44th in the world, and was on a par with the Cayman Islands ($1 927.1). The value added of industry per capita in Bermuda was greater than industry per capita in the world ($1 175.6) by 63.0%, and was less than industry per capita in the Americas ($2 704.1) by 29.1%.

The growth of industry in Bermuda was 2.4% in the 1990s, ranked 104th in the world, and was on a par with France (2.4%). The growth of industry in Bermuda (2.4%) was less than growth of industry in the world (2.5%), was less than growth of industry in the Americas (2.8%).

Comparison with neighbors. The value added of industry in Bermuda was less than in the USA ($1.5 trillion) and in the Bahamas ($369.7 million). The industry per capita in Bermuda was greater than in the Bahamas ($1 336.5); but less than in the USA ($5.7 thousand). The growth of industry in Bermuda was less than in the Bahamas (2.9%) and in the United States (2.8%).

Comparison with leaders. The sector of industry in Bermuda was less than in the United States ($1.5 trillion), in Japan ($1.2 trillion), in Germany ($534.0 billion), in China ($285.9 billion), and in the UK ($268.6 billion). The industry per capita in Bermuda was greater than in China ($231.9); but less than in Japan ($9.4 thousand), in Germany ($6.6 thousand), in the United States ($5.7 thousand), and in the UK ($4.6 thousand). The growth of industry in Bermuda was greater than in Japan (1.3%), in the UK (1.2%), and in Germany (0.33%); but less than in China (13.1%) and in the United States (2.8%).

The 2000s

The value of industry in Bermuda was $165.7 million per year in the 2000s, ranked 171st in the world. The share in the world was 0.0016%, and 0.0054% in the Americas.

The share of industry in the economy of Bermuda was 3.4% in the 2000s, ranked 205th in the world, and was on a par with the Virgin Islands (3.3%).

The value added of industry per capita in Bermuda was $2 517.7 in the 2000s, ranked 48th in the world, and was on a par with Greece ($2.5 thousand). The industry per capita in Bermuda was greater than industry per capita in the world ($1 573.8) by 60.0%, and was less than industry per capita in the Americas ($3 499.5) by 28.1%.

The growth of industry in Bermuda was -1.9% in the 2000s, ranked 199th in the world. The growth of industry in Bermuda (-1.9%) was less than growth of industry in the world (2.9%), was less than growth of industry in the Americas (1.4%).

Comparison with neighbors. The value of industry in Bermuda was less than in the United States ($2.1 trillion) and in the Bahamas ($519.9 million). The industry per capita in Bermuda was greater than in the Bahamas ($1 611.3); but less than in the United States ($7.1 thousand). The growth of industry in Bermuda was less than in the Bahamas (1.7%) and in the USA (1.5%).

Comparison with leaders. The Bermuda's industry was less than in the United States ($2.1 trillion), in Japan ($1.1 trillion), in China ($1.1 trillion), in Germany ($629.4 billion), and in the UK ($345.1 billion). The sector of industry per capita in Bermuda was greater than in China ($795.3); but less than in Japan ($8.8 thousand), in Germany ($7.7 thousand), in the USA ($7.1 thousand), and in the UK ($5.7 thousand). The growth of industry in Bermuda was less than in China (11.1%), in the USA (1.5%), in Germany (0.19%), in Japan (0.15%), and in the UK (-1.1%).

The 2010s

The sector of industry in Bermuda was $140.7 million per year in the 2010s, ranked 182nd in the world. The share in the world was 0.0008%, and 0.0033% in the Americas.

The share of industry in the economy of Bermuda was 2.2% in the 2010s, ranked 209th in the world.

The value added of industry per capita in Bermuda was $2 201.2 in the 2010s, ranked 69th in the world, and was on a par with Turkey ($2.2 thousand), the Caribbean ($2.2 thousand), Curaçao ($2.2 thousand). The value added of industry per capita in Bermuda was less than industry per capita in the world ($2 320.9) by 5.2%, and was less than industry per capita in the Americas ($4 354.8) by 49.5%.

The growth of industry in Bermuda was -5.2% in the 2010s, ranked 205th in the world, and was on a par with Equatorial Guinea (-5.2%), Sint Maarten (-5.2%). The growth of industry in Bermuda (-5.2%) was less than growth of industry in the world (3.5%), was less than growth of industry in the Americas (1.8%).

Comparison with neighbors. The value added of industry in Bermuda was 19 491.8 times lower than in the United States ($2.7 trillion) and 4.6 times lower than in the Bahamas ($653.3 million). The Bermuda's industry per capita was 25.5% higher than in the Bahamas ($1 753.9); but 3.9 times lower than in the USA ($8.6 thousand). The growth of industry in Bermuda was less than in the USA (2.2%) and in the Bahamas (1.7%).

Comparison with leaders. The value added of industry in Bermuda was 26 185.7 times lower than in China ($3.7 trillion), 19 491.8 times lower than in the United States ($2.7 trillion), 8 463.3 times lower than in Japan ($1.2 trillion), 5 971.8 times lower than in Germany ($840.0 billion), and 3 152.2 times lower than in India ($443.4 billion). The value of industry per capita in Bermuda was 6.5 times higher than in India ($340.6); but 4.7 times lower than in Germany ($10.3 thousand), 4.2 times lower than in Japan ($9.3 thousand), 3.9 times lower than in the USA ($8.6 thousand), and 16.2% lower than in China ($2.6 thousand). The growth of industry in Bermuda was less than in China (7.5%), in India (6.5%), in Germany (3.2%), in Japan (2.6%), and in the United States (2.2%).

Chapter 5.1. Manufacturing

(ISIC D)

The Bermuda's manufacturing increased from $11.4 million per year in the 1970s to $37.9 million per year in the 2010s, that is by $26.5 million or 3.3 times. The change occurred at $31.4 million due to a 5.8-fold increase in prices, as also at -$6.7 million due to a 2.0-fold decrease in productivity, as well as at $1.8 million due to the expansion in population. The average annual growth in manufacturing is -1.2%. The minimum value of manufacturing was in 1970 at $6.4 million. The maximum value of manufacturing was in 2006 at $90.0 million.

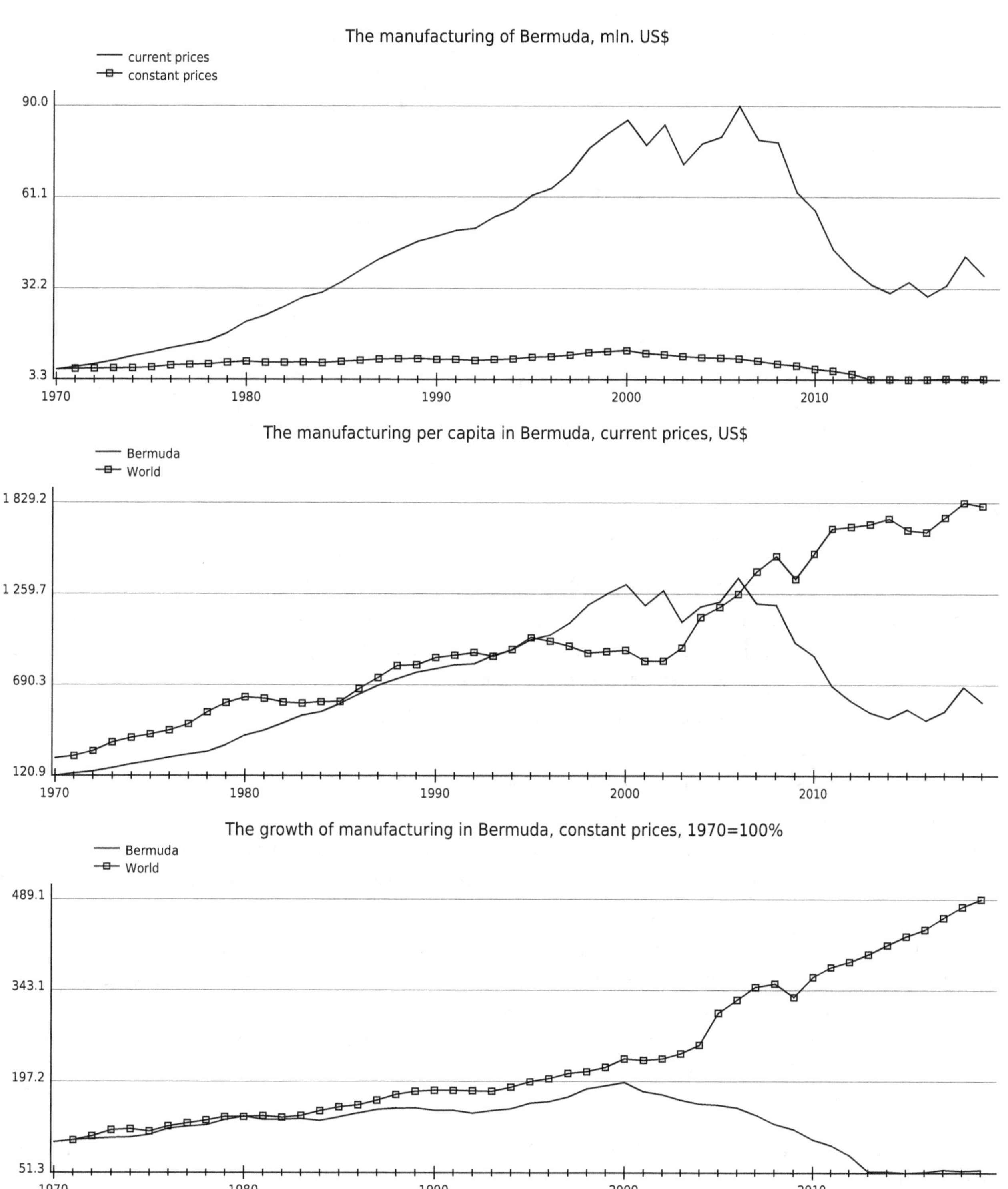

The manufacturing of Bermuda, mln. US$

The manufacturing per capita in Bermuda, current prices, US$

The growth of manufacturing in Bermuda, constant prices, 1970=100%

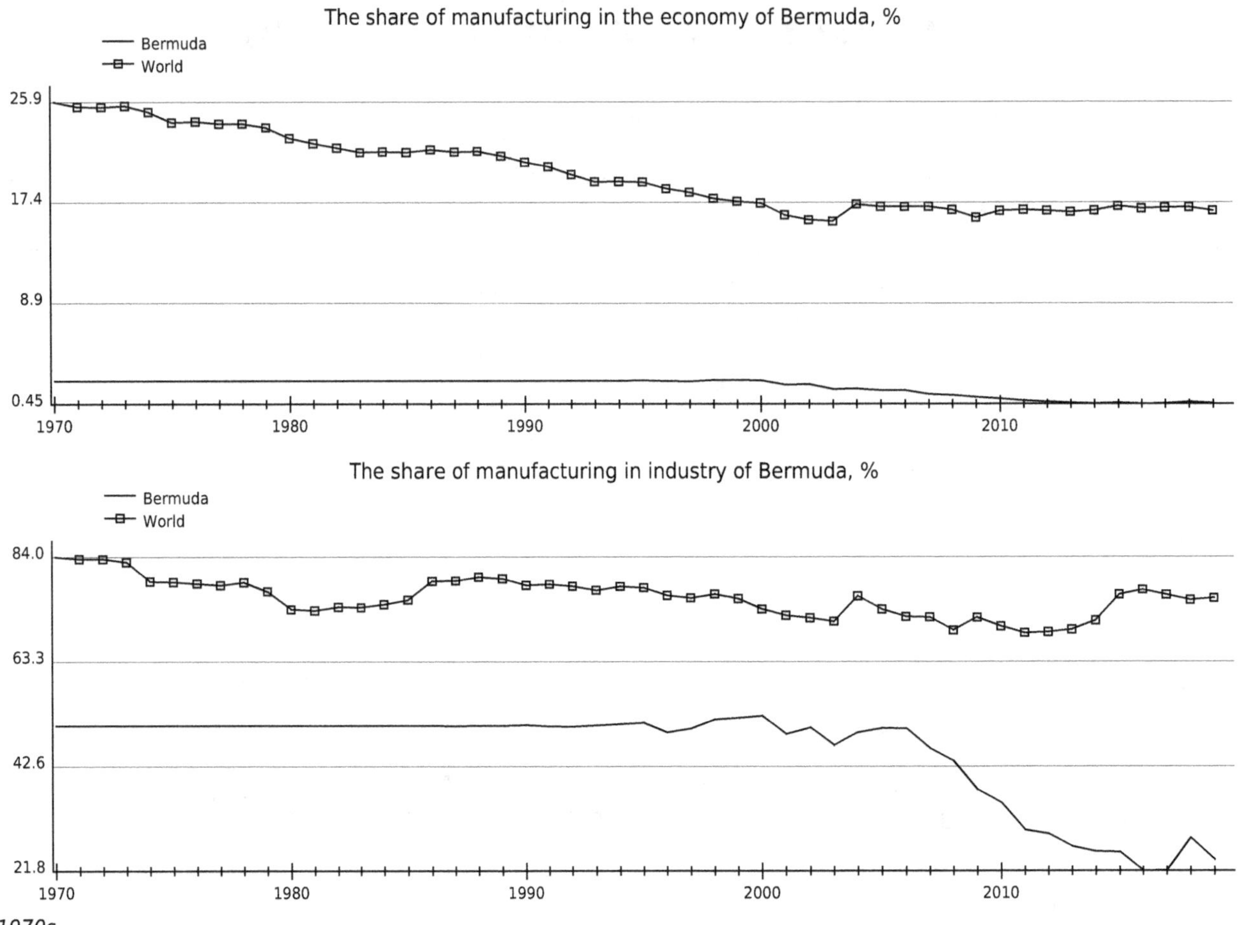

The 1970s

The value added of manufacturing in Bermuda was $11.4 million per year in the 1970s, ranked 148th in the world, and was on a par with Oman ($11.4 million). The share in the world was 0.0007%, and 0.0023% in the Americas.

The share of manufacturing in the economy of Bermuda was 2.4% in the 1970s, ranked 173rd in the world.

The manufacturing per capita in Bermuda was $207.5 in the 1970s, ranked 66th in the world, and was on a par with Gabon ($207.4), Panama ($203.7). The manufacturing per capita in Bermuda was less than manufacturing per capita in the world ($383.2) by 45.9%, and was less than manufacturing per capita in the Americas ($896.7) in 4.3 times.

The growth of manufacturing in Bermuda was 3.5% in the 1970s, ranked 124th in the world, and was on a par with Namibia (3.4%), Europe (3.5%), Zimbabwe (3.5%). The growth of manufacturing in Bermuda (3.5%) was less than growth of manufacturing in the world (3.8%), was less than growth of manufacturing in the Americas (3.6%).

Comparison with neighbors. The value added of manufacturing in Bermuda was less than in the USA ($378.0 billion) and in the Bahamas ($31.7 million). The value of manufacturing per capita in Bermuda was greater than in the Bahamas ($169.2); but less than in the USA ($1 731.8). The growth of manufacturing in Bermuda was greater than in the United States (2.7%) and in the Bahamas (2.4%).

Comparison with leaders. The value of manufacturing in Bermuda was less than in the USA ($378.0 billion), in the USSR ($248.8 billion), in Japan ($169.3 billion), in Germany ($138.0 billion), and in France ($64.5 billion). The manufacturing per capita in Bermuda was less than in Germany ($1 752.1), in the United States ($1 731.8), in Japan ($1 520.6), in France ($1 203.0), and in the USSR ($986.6). The growth of manufacturing in Bermuda was greater than in the USA (2.7%) and in Germany (2.1%); but less than in the USSR (5.2%), in Japan (4.5%), and in France (3.5%).

The 1980s

The Bermudian manufacturing was $33.7 million per year in the 1980s, ranked 148th in the world. The share in the world was 0.0011%, and 0.0032% in the Americas.

The share of manufacturing in the economy of Bermuda was 2.4% in the 1980s, ranked 175th in the world.

The manufacturing per capita in Bermuda was $567.3 in the 1980s, ranked 53rd in the world, and was on a par with Uruguay ($554.7). The manufacturing per capita in Bermuda was less than manufacturing per capita in the world ($661.2) by 14.2%, and was less than manufacturing per capita in the Americas ($1 597.5) in 2.8 times.

The growth of manufacturing in Bermuda was 1.3% in the 1980s, ranked 136th in the world, and was on a par with Micronesia (1.3%). The growth of manufacturing in Bermuda (1.3%) was less than growth of manufacturing in the world (2.6%), was less than growth of manufacturing in the Americas (1.8%).

Comparison with neighbors. The manufacturing of Bermuda was less than in the United States ($789.4 billion) and in the Bahamas ($87.8 million). The Bermuda's manufacturing per capita was greater than in the Bahamas ($379.1); but less than in the United States ($3.3 thousand). The growth of manufacturing in Bermuda was less than in the Bahamas (4.4%) and in the United States (1.9%).

Comparison with leaders. The manufacturing of Bermuda was less than in the USA ($789.4 billion), in Japan ($501.0 billion), in the USSR ($305.7 billion), in Germany ($258.7 billion), and in Italy ($134.1 billion). The manufacturing per capita in Bermuda was less than in Japan ($4.1 thousand), in Germany ($3.3 thousand), in the United States ($3.3 thousand), in Italy ($2.4 thousand), and in the USSR ($1 110.8). The growth of manufacturing in Bermuda was greater than in Germany (1.2%); but less than in the USSR (5.3%), in Japan (4.4%), in Italy (2.5%), and in the USA (1.9%).

The 1990s

The sector of manufacturing in Bermuda was $61.6 million per year in the 1990s, ranked 168th in the world. The share in the world was 0.0012%, and 0.0037% in the Americas.

The share of manufacturing in the economy of Bermuda was 2.4% in the 1990s, ranked 197th in the world.

The value added of manufacturing per capita in Bermuda was $973.5 in the 1990s, ranked 48th in the world, and was on a par with Turkey ($970.4), Mexico ($979.6), Malaysia ($990.2). The sector of manufacturing per capita in Bermuda was greater than manufacturing per capita in the world ($908.4) by 7.2%, and was less than manufacturing per capita in the Americas ($2 172.9) in 2.2 times.

The growth of manufacturing in Bermuda was 2.1% in the 1990s, ranked 109th in the world. The growth of manufacturing in Bermuda (2.1%) was greater than growth of manufacturing in the world (2.0%), was less than growth of manufacturing in the Americas (3.0%).

Comparison with neighbors. The value added of manufacturing in Bermuda was less than in the USA ($1.2 trillion) and in the Bahamas ($138.0 million). The value added of manufacturing per capita in Bermuda was greater than in the Bahamas ($498.8); but less than in the United States ($4.7 thousand). The growth of manufacturing in Bermuda was less than in the USA (3.2%) and in the Bahamas (3.0%).

Comparison with leaders. The value of manufacturing in Bermuda was less than in the United States ($1.2 trillion), in Japan ($1.0 trillion), in Germany ($468.8 billion), in Italy ($227.8 billion), and in France ($215.0 billion). The sector of manufacturing per capita in Bermuda was less than in Japan ($8.3 thousand), in Germany ($5.8 thousand), in the USA ($4.7 thousand), in Italy ($4.0 thousand), and in France ($3.6 thousand). The growth of manufacturing in Bermuda was greater than in Italy (1.2%), in Japan (1.1%), and in Germany (0.26%); but less than in the USA (3.2%) and in France (2.4%).

The 2000s

The sector of manufacturing in Bermuda was $78.7 million per year in the 2000s, ranked 173rd in the world, and was on a par with the Seychelles ($80.2 million). The share in the world was 0.0011%, and 0.0035% in the Americas.

The share of manufacturing in the economy of Bermuda was 1.6% in the 2000s, ranked 205th in the world.

The manufacturing per capita in Bermuda was $1 196.1 in the 2000s, ranked 56th in the world. The value added of manufacturing per capita in Bermuda was greater than manufacturing per capita in the world ($1 138.1) by 5.1%, and was less than manufacturing per capita in the Americas ($2 583.7) in 2.2 times.

The growth of manufacturing in Bermuda was -4.5% in the 2000s, ranked 201st in the world. The growth of manufacturing in Bermuda (-4.5%) was less than growth of manufacturing in the world (4.2%), was less than growth of manufacturing in the Americas (1.4%).

Comparison with neighbors. The Bermudian manufacturing was less than in the United States ($1.6 trillion) and in the Bahamas

($226.4 million). The value added of manufacturing per capita in Bermuda was greater than in the Bahamas ($701.6); but less than in the United States ($5.6 thousand). The growth of manufacturing in Bermuda was less than in the USA (1.6%) and in the Bahamas (-0.19%).

Comparison with leaders. The Bermuda's manufacturing was less than in the USA ($1.6 trillion), in China ($1.1 trillion), in Japan ($992.9 billion), in Germany ($551.4 billion), and in Italy ($277.2 billion). The value of manufacturing per capita in Bermuda was greater than in China ($815.3); but less than in Japan ($7.7 thousand), in Germany ($6.8 thousand), in the United States ($5.6 thousand), and in Italy ($4.8 thousand). The growth of manufacturing in Bermuda was less than in the United States (1.6%), in Japan (0.32%), in Germany (0.097%), and in Italy (-1.3%).

The 2010s

The sector of manufacturing in Bermuda was $37.9 million per year in the 2010s, ranked 190th in the world. The share in the world was 0.0003%, and 0.0013% in the Americas.

The share of manufacturing in the economy of Bermuda was 0.59% in the 2010s, ranked 210th in the world.

The Bermuda's manufacturing per capita was $593.6 in the 2010s, ranked 102nd in the world, and was on a par with Lebanon ($599.6), El Salvador ($587.6), Tunisia ($607.6). The value of manufacturing per capita in Bermuda was less than manufacturing per capita in the world ($1 697.4) in 2.9 times, and was less than manufacturing per capita in the Americas ($3 100.6) in 5.2 times.

The growth of manufacturing in Bermuda was -7.4% in the 2010s, ranked 209th in the world. The growth of manufacturing in Bermuda (-7.4%) was less than growth of manufacturing in the world (3.9%), was less than growth of manufacturing in the Americas (1.6%).

Comparison with neighbors. The manufacturing of Bermuda was 54 586.6 times lower than in the USA ($2.1 trillion) and 7.9 times lower than in the Bahamas ($299.7 million). The manufacturing per capita in Bermuda was 10.9 times lower than in the USA ($6.5 thousand) and 26.2% lower than in the Bahamas ($804.6). The growth of manufacturing in Bermuda was less than in the United States (1.9%) and in the Bahamas (-0.61%).

Comparison with leaders. The Bermudian manufacturing was 82 125.5 times lower than in China ($3.1 trillion), 54 586.6 times lower than in the USA ($2.1 trillion), 27 945.4 times lower than in Japan ($1.1 trillion), 19 382.3 times lower than in Germany ($735.2 billion), and 10 295.4 times lower than in Republic of Korea ($390.5 billion). The sector of manufacturing per capita in Bermuda was 15.1 times lower than in Germany ($9.0 thousand), 14.0 times lower than in Japan ($8.3 thousand), 13.0 times lower than in South Korea ($7.7 thousand), 10.9 times lower than in the United States ($6.5 thousand), and 3.7 times lower than in China ($2.2 thousand). The growth of manufacturing in Bermuda was less than in China (7.5%), in Republic of Korea (3.8%), in Germany (3.5%), in Japan (3.0%), and in the United States (1.9%).

Chapter VI. Construction

(ISIC F)

The value of construction in Bermuda rose from $26.6 million per year in the 1970s to $231.9 million per year in the 2010s, that is by $205.3 million or 8.7 times. The change occurred at $196.9 million due to a 6.6-fold increase in prices, as also at $4.2 million due to a 1.1-fold increase in productivity, as well as at $4.3 million due to the growth in population. The average annual growth in construction is 1.3%. The minimum value of construction was in 1970 at $14.8 million. The maximum value of construction was in 2008 at $381.7 million.

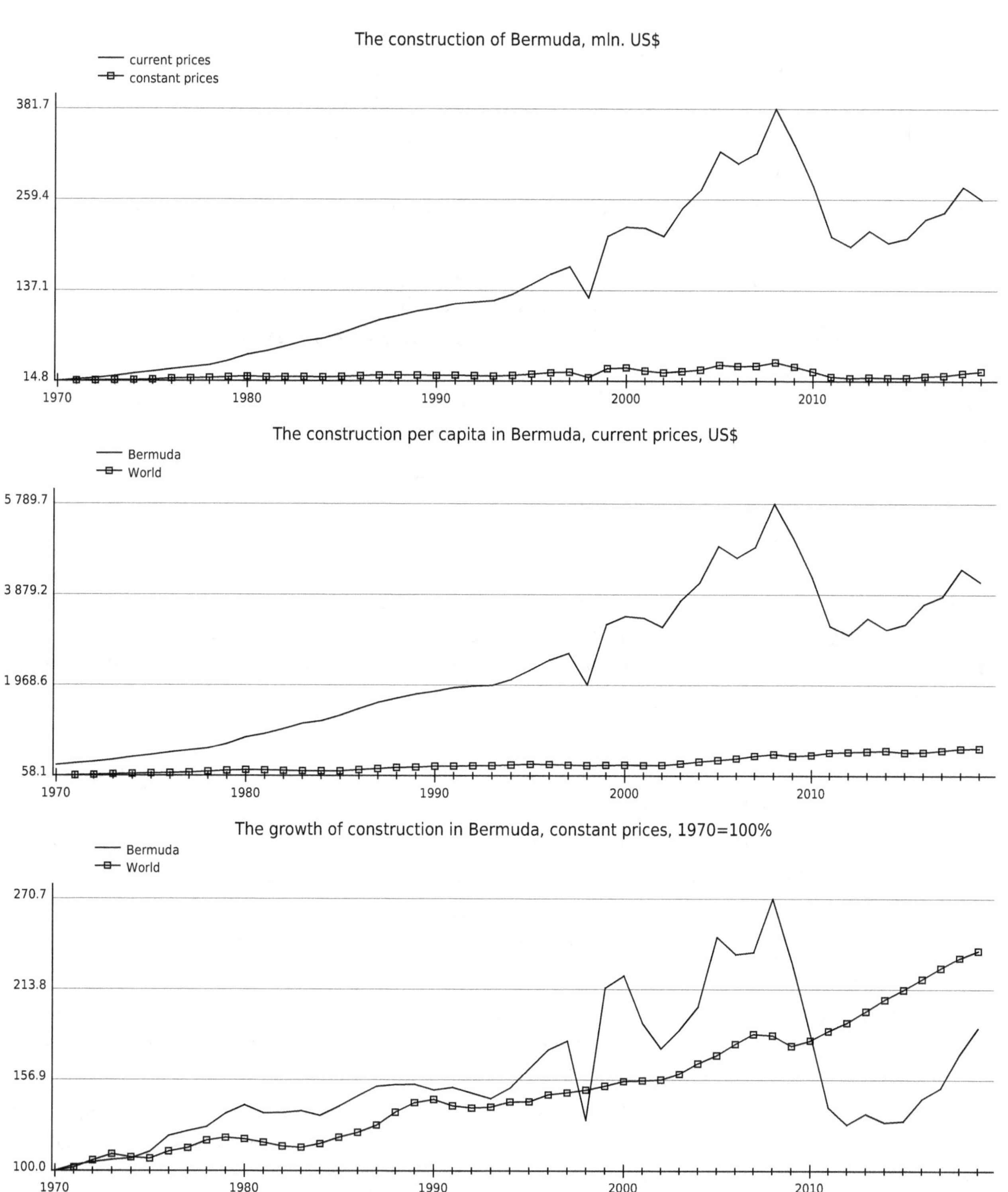

The construction of Bermuda, mln. US$

The construction per capita in Bermuda, current prices, US$

The growth of construction in Bermuda, constant prices, 1970=100%

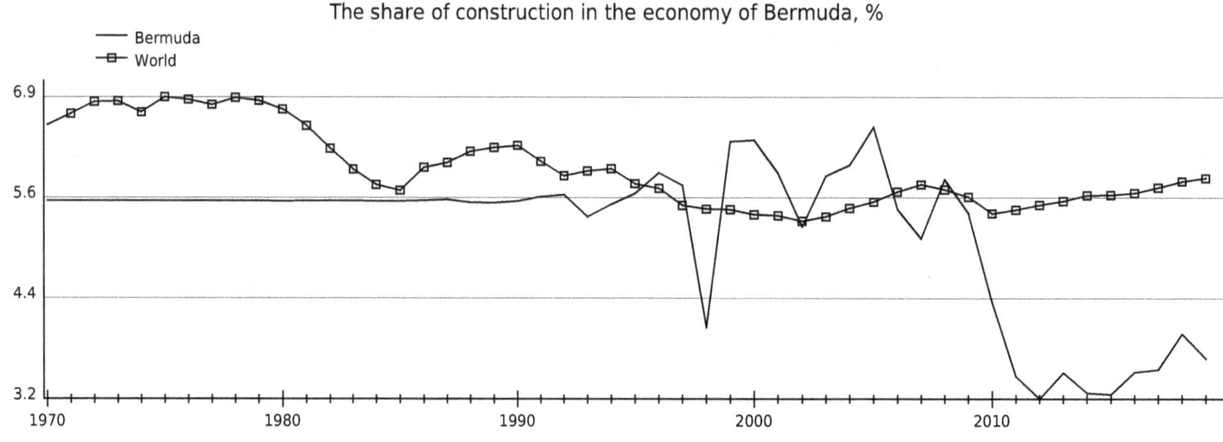

The 1970s

The construction of Bermuda was $26.6 million per year in the 1970s, ranked 131st in the world, and was on a par with Somalia ($26.6 million). The share in the world was 0.0062%, and 0.022% in the Americas.

The share of construction in the economy of Bermuda was 5.6% in the 1970s, ranked 107th in the world, and was on a par with Saint Lucia (5.6%), Bolivia (5.6%), Antigua and Barbuda (5.6%).

The Bermuda's construction per capita was $482.7 in the 1970s, ranked 16th in the world, and was on a par with the Netherlands ($479.7), Saudi Arabia ($489.5), Denmark ($475.2). The Bermudian construction per capita was greater than construction per capita in the world ($106.1) in 4.5 times, and was greater than construction per capita in the Americas ($217.5) in 2.2 times.

The growth of construction in Bermuda was 3.5% in the 1970s, ranked 109th in the world, and was on a par with Portugal (3.4%). The growth of construction in Bermuda (3.5%) was greater than growth of construction in the world (2.1%), was greater than growth of construction in the Americas (1.5%).

Comparison with neighbors. The sector of construction in Bermuda was less than in the United States ($81.1 billion) and in the Bahamas ($67.3 million). The construction per capita in Bermuda was greater than in the USA ($371.5) and in the Bahamas ($359.1). The growth of construction in Bermuda was greater than in the Bahamas (2.4%) and in the USA (0.31%).

Comparison with leaders. The Bermudian construction was less than in the United States ($81.1 billion), in the USSR ($52.5 billion), in Japan ($43.5 billion), in Germany ($33.8 billion), and in France ($22.4 billion). The sector of construction per capita in Bermuda was greater than in Germany ($428.6), in France ($417.3), in Japan ($390.8), in the USA ($371.5), and in the USSR ($208.1). The growth of construction in Bermuda was greater than in Japan (3.4%), in France (2.0%), in Germany (0.66%), and in the United States (0.31%); but less than in the USSR (6.5%).

The 1980s

The value added of construction in Bermuda was $78.4 million per year in the 1980s, ranked 122nd in the world, and was on a par with Congo ($80.1 million), Rwanda ($80.1 million). The share in the world was 0.0087%, and 0.030% in the Americas.

The share of construction in the economy of Bermuda was 5.6% in the 1980s, ranked 90th in the world, and was on a par with Africa (5.6%), Eswatini (5.6%), Luxembourg (5.5%).

The sector of construction per capita in Bermuda was $1 319.2 in the 1980s, ranked 8th in the world. The Bermuda's construction per capita was greater than construction per capita in the world ($186.2) in 7.1 times, and was greater than construction per capita in the Americas ($396.8) in 3.3 times.

The growth of construction in Bermuda was 1.3% in the 1980s, ranked 110th in the world, and was on a par with Northern America (1.3%). The growth of construction in Bermuda (1.3%) was less than growth of construction in the world (1.7%), was greater than growth of construction in the Americas (0.83%).

Comparison with neighbors. The construction of Bermuda was less than in the USA ($180.6 billion) and in the Bahamas ($187.4 million). The construction per capita in Bermuda was greater than in the Bahamas ($808.6) and in the USA ($754.4). The growth of construction in Bermuda was greater than in the USA (1.1%); but less than in the Bahamas (4.3%).

Comparison with leaders. The sector of construction in Bermuda was less than in the United States ($180.6 billion), in Japan ($138.7 billion), in the USSR ($72.1 billion), in Germany ($57.8 billion), and in France ($42.5 billion). The sector of construction per capita in Bermuda was greater than in Japan ($1 143.9), in the United States ($754.4), in France ($751.9), in Germany ($740.2), and in the USSR ($262.0). The growth of construction in Bermuda was greater than in the United States (1.1%), in France (0.67%), and in Germany (-0.52%); but less than in the USSR (6.2%) and in Japan (2.1%).

The 1990s

The sector of construction in Bermuda was $141.9 million per year in the 1990s, ranked 136th in the world, and was on a par with Andorra ($141.7 million), Myanmar ($145.3 million). The share in the world was 0.0089%, and 0.033% in the Americas.

The share of construction in the economy of Bermuda was 5.6% in the 1990s, ranked 109th in the world, and was on a par with Canada (5.6%), Kyrgyzstan (5.6%), Vietnam (5.6%).

The Bermuda's construction per capita was $2 243.6 in the 1990s, ranked 9th in the world. The sector of construction per capita in Bermuda was greater than construction per capita in the world ($278.6) in 8.1 times, and was greater than construction per capita in the Americas ($564.1) in 4.0 times.

The growth of construction in Bermuda was 3.4% in the 1990s, ranked 94th in the world, and was on a par with Austria (3.3%). The growth of construction in Bermuda (3.4%) was greater than growth of construction in the world (0.71%), was greater than growth of construction in the Americas (1.8%).

Comparison with neighbors. The construction of Bermuda was less than in the USA ($299.1 billion) and in the Bahamas ($280.8 million). The value added of construction per capita in Bermuda was greater than in the USA ($1 131.2) and in the Bahamas ($1 015.0). The growth of construction in Bermuda was greater than in the United States (1.8%) and in the Bahamas (-8.1%).

Comparison with leaders. The sector of construction in Bermuda was less than in Japan ($343.2 billion), in the United States ($299.1 billion), in Germany ($125.2 billion), in the United Kingdom ($69.8 billion), and in France ($68.8 billion). The value added of construction per capita in Bermuda was greater than in Germany ($1 552.3), in the UK ($1 205.1), in France ($1 158.8), and in the USA ($1 131.2); but less than in Japan ($2.7 thousand). The growth of construction in Bermuda was greater than in the United States (1.8%), in Germany (-0.047%), in the United Kingdom (-0.34%), in France (-0.65%), and in Japan (-1.0%).

The 2000s

The Bermuda's construction was $284.2 million per year in the 2000s, ranked 137th in the world, and was on a par with Chad ($281.0 million), Polynesia ($280.9 million), Moldova ($288.1 million). The share in the world was 0.011%, and 0.035% in the Americas.

The share of construction in the economy of Bermuda was 5.8% in the 2000s, ranked 106th in the world, and was on a par with Papua New Guinea (5.8%), Italy (5.7%), Morocco (5.7%).

The Bermuda's construction per capita was $4 316.9 in the 2000s, ranked 3rd in the world. The value of construction per capita in Bermuda was greater than construction per capita in the world ($381.3) in 11.3 times, and was greater than construction per capita in the Americas ($931.0) in 4.6 times.

The growth of construction in Bermuda was 0.8% in the 2000s, ranked 174th in the world. The growth of construction in Bermuda (0.77%) was less than growth of construction in the world (1.5%), was greater than growth of construction in the Americas (-0.96%).

Comparison with neighbors. The value added of construction in Bermuda was less than in the United States ($583.0 billion) and in the Bahamas ($475.1 million). The construction per capita in Bermuda was greater than in the USA ($1 983.7) and in the Bahamas ($1 472.3). The growth of construction in Bermuda was greater than in the United States (-2.6%); but less than in the Bahamas (2.6%).

Comparison with leaders. The value added of construction in Bermuda was less than in the USA ($583.0 billion), in Japan ($270.5 billion), in China ($150.1 billion), in the UK ($132.1 billion), and in Spain ($111.8 billion). The sector of construction per capita in Bermuda was greater than in Spain ($2.6 thousand), in the United Kingdom ($2.2 thousand), in Japan ($2.1 thousand), in the United States ($1 983.7), and in China ($113.1). The growth of construction in Bermuda was greater than in the UK (0.17%), in the United States (-2.6%), and in Japan (-3.9%); but less than in China (11.9%) and in Spain (1.7%).

The 2010s

The value of construction in Bermuda was $231.9 million per year in the 2010s, ranked 163rd in the world, and was on a par with

Montenegro ($227.6 million). The share in the world was 0.0055%, and 0.020% in the Americas.

The share of construction in the economy of Bermuda was 3.6% in the 2010s, ranked 180th in the world, and was on a par with Sudan (3.6%).

The sector of construction per capita in Bermuda was $3 628.8 in the 2010s, ranked 10th in the world, and was on a par with the UAE ($3.6 thousand). The sector of construction per capita in Bermuda was greater than construction per capita in the world ($572.1) in 6.3 times, and was greater than construction per capita in the Americas ($1 189.0) in 3.1 times.

The growth of construction in Bermuda was -2% in the 2010s, ranked 182nd in the world. The growth of construction in Bermuda (-2.0%) was less than growth of construction in the world (2.9%), was less than growth of construction in the Americas (1.3%).

Comparison with neighbors. The construction of Bermuda was 2 936.0 times lower than in the USA ($680.8 billion) and 3.5 times lower than in the Bahamas ($806.7 million). The value of construction per capita in Bermuda was 67.6% higher than in the Bahamas ($2.2 thousand) and 70.3% higher than in the United States ($2.1 thousand). The growth of construction in Bermuda was less than in the Bahamas (15.8%) and in the USA (1.4%).

Comparison with leaders. The Bermuda's construction was 3 152.9 times lower than in China ($731.1 billion), 2 936.0 times lower than in the USA ($680.8 billion), 1 201.7 times lower than in Japan ($278.7 billion), 724.9 times lower than in India ($168.1 billion), and 660.8 times lower than in Germany ($153.2 billion). The value of construction per capita in Bermuda was 66.6% higher than in Japan ($2.2 thousand), 70.3% higher than in the USA ($2.1 thousand), 93.9% higher than in Germany ($1 871.9), 7.0 times higher than in China ($521.3), and 28.1 times higher than in India ($129.1). The growth of construction in Bermuda was less than in China (8.2%), in India (5.2%), in Germany (1.8%), in Japan (1.7%), and in the USA (1.4%).

Chapter VII. Transportation

Transport, storage and communication (ISIC I)

The transportation of Bermuda grew up from $34.1 million per year in the 1970s to $330.9 million per year in the 2010s, that is by $296.8 million or 9.7 times. The change occurred at $277.0 million due to a 6.1-fold increase in prices, as also at $14.2 million due to a 1.4-fold increase in productivity, as well as at $5.5 million due to the growing in population. The average annual growth in transportation is 1.1%. The minimum value of transportation was in 1970 at $19.0 million. The maximum value of transportation was in 2018 at $364.9 million.

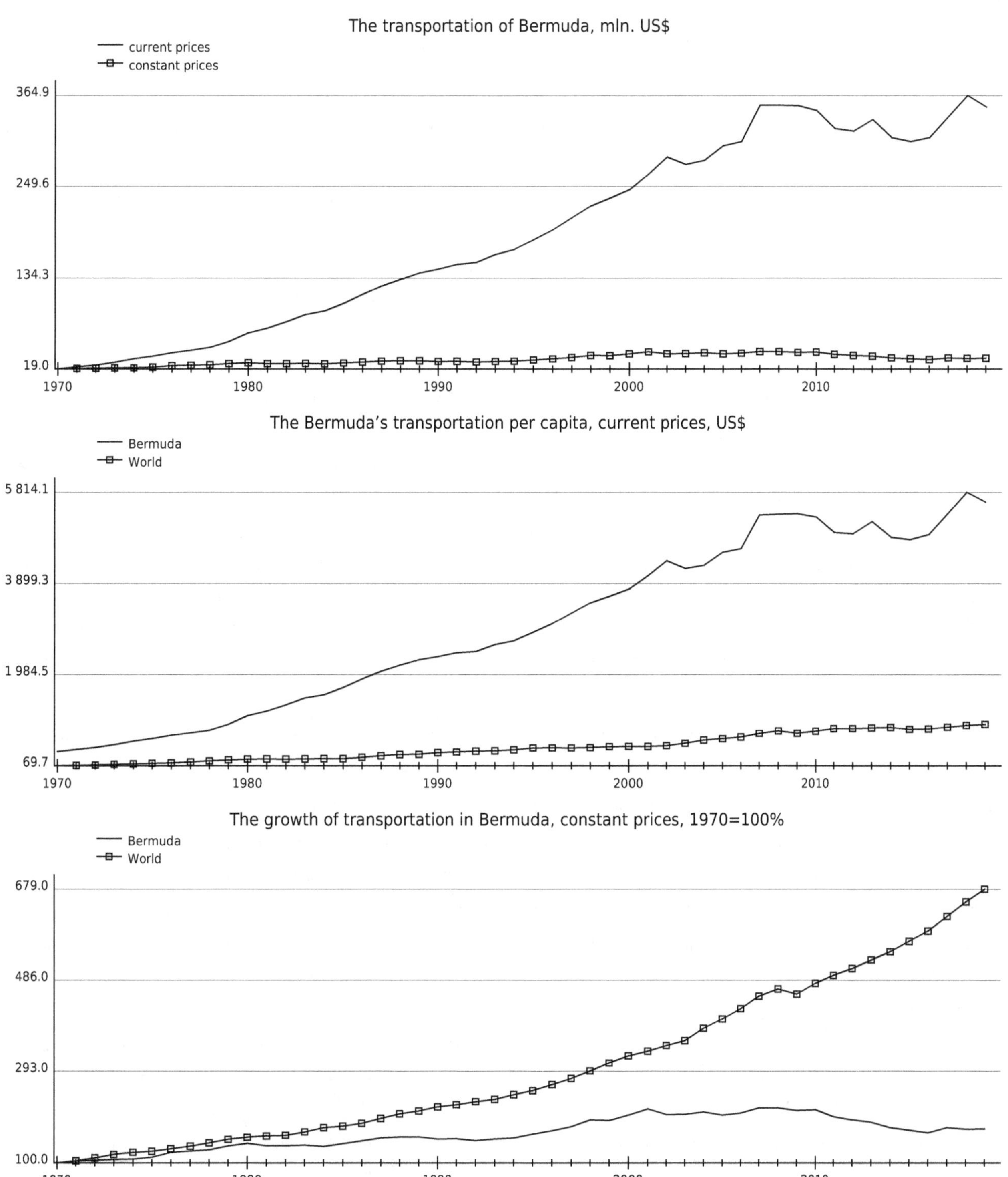

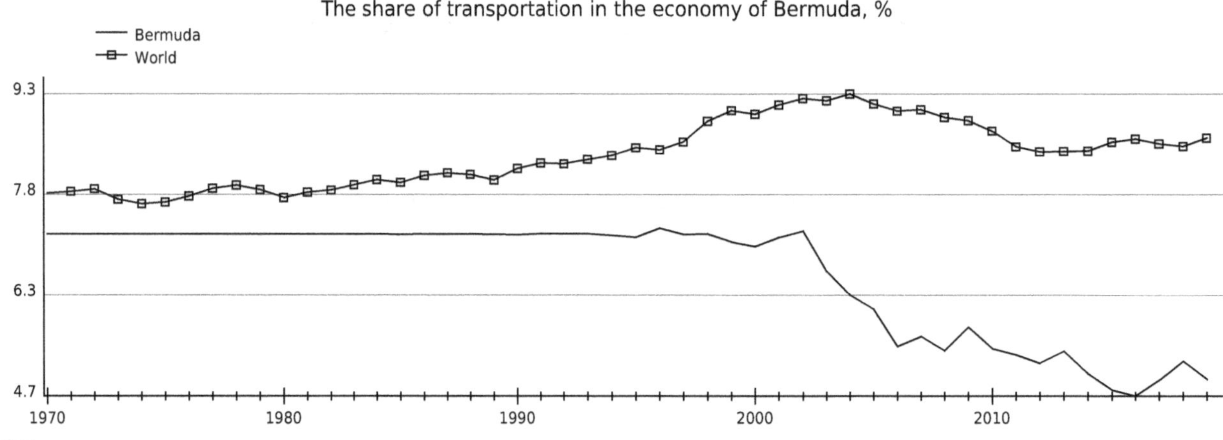

The 1970s

The transportation of Bermuda was $34.1 million per year in the 1970s, ranked 125th in the world, and was on a par with Suriname ($33.4 million), Niger ($35.0 million). The share in the world was 0.0069%, and 0.017% in the Americas.

The share of transportation in the economy of Bermuda was 7.2% in the 1970s, ranked 88th in the world, and was on a par with Republic of Korea (7.2%).

The Bermuda's transportation per capita was $620.3 in the 1970s, ranked 10th in the world. The Bermudian transportation per capita was greater than transportation per capita in the world ($122.3) in 5.1 times, and was greater than transportation per capita in the Americas ($360.9) by 71.9%.

The growth of transportation in Bermuda was 3.5% in the 1970s, ranked 136th in the world. The growth of transportation in Bermuda (3.5%) was less than growth of transportation in the world (4.6%), was less than growth of transportation in the Americas (4.9%).

Comparison with neighbors. The Bermudian transportation was less than in the USA ($168.6 billion) and in the Bahamas ($66.7 million). The value of transportation per capita in Bermuda was greater than in the Bahamas ($356.1); but less than in the USA ($772.4). The growth of transportation in Bermuda was greater than in the Bahamas (2.4%); but less than in the United States (4.2%).

Comparison with leaders. The value added of transportation in Bermuda was less than in the United States ($168.6 billion), in Japan ($46.4 billion), in Germany ($29.6 billion), in the USSR ($28.8 billion), and in France ($24.0 billion). The value added of transportation per capita in Bermuda was greater than in France ($447.4), in Japan ($416.6), in Germany ($376.1), and in the USSR ($114.0); but less than in the United States ($772.4). The growth of transportation in Bermuda was greater than in Germany (3.0%) and in Japan (1.7%); but less than in the USSR (8.1%), in the USA (4.2%), and in France (4.1%).

The 1980s

The transportation of Bermuda was $100.7 million per year in the 1980s, ranked 119th in the world, and was on a par with Mongolia ($100.3 million), Benin ($99.9 million). The share in the world was 0.0086%, and 0.021% in the Americas.

The share of transportation in the economy of Bermuda was 7.2% in the 1980s, ranked 98th in the world.

The transportation per capita in Bermuda was $1 695.9 in the 1980s, ranked 6th in the world, and was on a par with Norway ($1 735.9). The sector of transportation per capita in Bermuda was greater than transportation per capita in the world ($242.0) in 7.0 times, and was greater than transportation per capita in the Americas ($714.8) in 2.4 times.

The growth of transportation in Bermuda was 1.3% in the 1980s, ranked 154th in the world, and was on a par with Kiribati (1.3%), Gabon (1.3%). The growth of transportation in Bermuda (1.3%) was less than growth of transportation in the world (3.4%), was less than growth of transportation in the Americas (3.5%).

Comparison with neighbors. The transportation of Bermuda was less than in the United States ($394.9 billion) and in the Bahamas ($191.9 million). The transportation per capita in Bermuda was greater than in the USA ($1 649.2) and in the Bahamas ($828.0). The growth of transportation in Bermuda was less than in the Bahamas (4.3%) and in the USA (3.6%).

Comparison with leaders. The value of transportation in Bermuda was less than in the USA ($394.9 billion), in Japan ($147.7 billion), in Germany ($56.6 billion), in France ($56.2 billion), and in the UK ($53.0 billion). The value of transportation per capita in Bermuda was greater than in the United States ($1 649.2), in Japan ($1 217.8), in France ($993.7), in the United Kingdom ($938.7), and in Germany ($725.5). The growth of transportation in Bermuda was less than in France (5.4%), in Japan (4.7%), in the USA (3.6%), in the United Kingdom (3.0%), and in Germany (1.8%).

The 1990s

The transportation of Bermuda was $183.2 million per year in the 1990s, ranked 134th in the world, and was on a par with Mali ($182.1 million), Fiji ($179.8 million), Afghanistan ($178.9 million). The share in the world was 0.0079%, and 0.022% in the Americas.

The share of transportation in the economy of Bermuda was 7.2% in the 1990s, ranked 124th in the world, and was on a par with Chad (7.2%), Kenya (7.2%), Equatorial Guinea (7.2%).

The Bermudian transportation per capita was $2 898.2 in the 1990s, ranked 8th in the world, and was on a par with Japan ($3.0 thousand). The sector of transportation per capita in Bermuda was greater than transportation per capita in the world ($409.5) in 7.1 times, and was greater than transportation per capita in the Americas ($1 104.4) in 2.6 times.

The growth of transportation in Bermuda was 2.1% in the 1990s, ranked 154th in the world. The growth of transportation in Bermuda (2.1%) was less than growth of transportation in the world (4.0%), was less than growth of transportation in the Americas (4.7%).

Comparison with neighbors. The sector of transportation in Bermuda was less than in the USA ($702.6 billion) and in the Bahamas ($331.8 million). The value of transportation per capita in Bermuda was greater than in the United States ($2.7 thousand) and in the Bahamas ($1 199.4). The growth of transportation in Bermuda was greater than in the Bahamas (1.4%); but less than in the USA (5.0%).

Comparison with leaders. The Bermudian transportation was less than in the United States ($702.6 billion), in Japan ($373.9 billion), in Germany ($144.3 billion), in France ($118.7 billion), and in the United Kingdom ($117.6 billion). The value of transportation per capita in Bermuda was greater than in the United States ($2.7 thousand), in the UK ($2.0 thousand), in France ($1 999.2), and in Germany ($1 789.0); but less than in Japan ($3.0 thousand). The growth of transportation in Bermuda was less than in the USA (5.0%), in France (4.8%), in the UK (4.7%), in Germany (3.9%), and in Japan (3.0%).

The 2000s

The Bermudian transportation was $302.6 million per year in the 2000s, ranked 144th in the world. The share in the world was 0.0075%, and 0.020% in the Americas.

The share of transportation in the economy of Bermuda was 6.1% in the 2000s, ranked 172nd in the world.

The value added of transportation per capita in Bermuda was $4 597.0 in the 2000s, ranked 5th in the world, and was on a par with Sweden ($4.5 thousand). The sector of transportation per capita in Bermuda was greater than transportation per capita in the world ($621.1) in 7.4 times, and was greater than transportation per capita in the Americas ($1 687.7) in 2.7 times.

The growth of transportation in Bermuda was 1.1% in the 2000s, ranked 190th in the world, and was on a par with Eritrea (1.1%). The growth of transportation in Bermuda (1.1%) was less than growth of transportation in the world (3.9%), was less than growth of transportation in the Americas (3.2%).

Comparison with neighbors. The sector of transportation in Bermuda was less than in the USA ($1.2 trillion) and in the Bahamas ($663.6 million). The Bermudian transportation per capita was greater than in the USA ($4.0 thousand) and in the Bahamas ($2.1 thousand). The growth of transportation in Bermuda was less than in the USA (3.1%) and in the Bahamas (1.4%).

Comparison with leaders. The value of transportation in Bermuda was less than in the United States ($1.2 trillion), in Japan ($468.5 billion), in Germany ($228.2 billion), in the United Kingdom ($215.9 billion), and in France ($185.6 billion). The value added of transportation per capita in Bermuda was greater than in the United States ($4.0 thousand), in Japan ($3.7 thousand), in the United Kingdom ($3.6 thousand), in France ($3.0 thousand), and in Germany ($2.8 thousand). The growth of transportation in Bermuda was less than in Germany (3.4%), in the United Kingdom (3.1%), in the United States (3.1%), in France (2.7%), and in Japan (1.5%).

The 2010s

The value added of transportation in Bermuda was $330.9 million per year in the 2010s, ranked 163rd in the world, and was on a par with Greenland ($327.6 million), Curaçao ($325.6 million). The share in the world was 0.0052%, and 0.014% in the Americas.

The share of transportation in the economy of Bermuda was 5.1% in the 2010s, ranked 187th in the world, and was on a par with

Equatorial Guinea (5.1%), Namibia (5.1%), Oman (5.1%).

The value added of transportation per capita in Bermuda was $5 178.2 in the 2010s, ranked 12th in the world, and was on a par with Denmark ($5.1 thousand). The Bermuda's transportation per capita was greater than transportation per capita in the world ($864.8) in 6.0 times, and was greater than transportation per capita in the Americas ($2 381.9) in 2.2 times.

The growth of transportation in Bermuda was -2% in the 2010s, ranked 202nd in the world. The growth of transportation in Bermuda (-2.0%) was less than growth of transportation in the world (4.0%), was less than growth of transportation in the Americas (4.7%).

Comparison with neighbors. The Bermudian transportation was 5 405.0 times lower than in the United States ($1.8 trillion) and 2.8 times lower than in the Bahamas ($919.0 million). The Bermudian transportation per capita was 2.1 times higher than in the Bahamas ($2.5 thousand); but 7.5% lower than in the USA ($5.6 thousand). The growth of transportation in Bermuda was less than in the United States (5.1%) and in the Bahamas (0.34%).

Comparison with leaders. The value added of transportation in Bermuda was 5 405.0 times lower than in the United States ($1.8 trillion), 1 601.3 times lower than in Japan ($529.8 billion), 1 403.0 times lower than in China ($464.2 billion), 906.7 times lower than in Germany ($300.0 billion), and 779.0 times lower than in the UK ($257.7 billion). The sector of transportation per capita in Bermuda was 25.0% higher than in Japan ($4.1 thousand), 31.8% higher than in the UK ($3.9 thousand), 41.3% higher than in Germany ($3.7 thousand), and 15.6 times higher than in China ($331.0); but 7.5% lower than in the USA ($5.6 thousand). The growth of transportation in Bermuda was less than in China (7.5%), in the USA (5.1%), in the UK (2.8%), in Germany (2.7%), and in Japan (0.81%).

Chapter VIII. Trade

Wholesale, retail trade, restaurants and hotels (ISIC G-H)

The trade of Bermuda rose from $83.7 million per year in the 1970s to $653.8 million per year in the 2010s, that is by $570.0 million or 7.8 times. The change occurred at $563.3 million due to a 7.2-fold increase in prices, as also at -$6.8 million due to a 1.1-fold decrease in productivity, as well as at $13.5 million due to the increase in population. The average annual growth in trade is 0.48%. The minimum value of trade was in 1970 at $46.6 million. The maximum value of trade was in 2018 at $752.2 million.

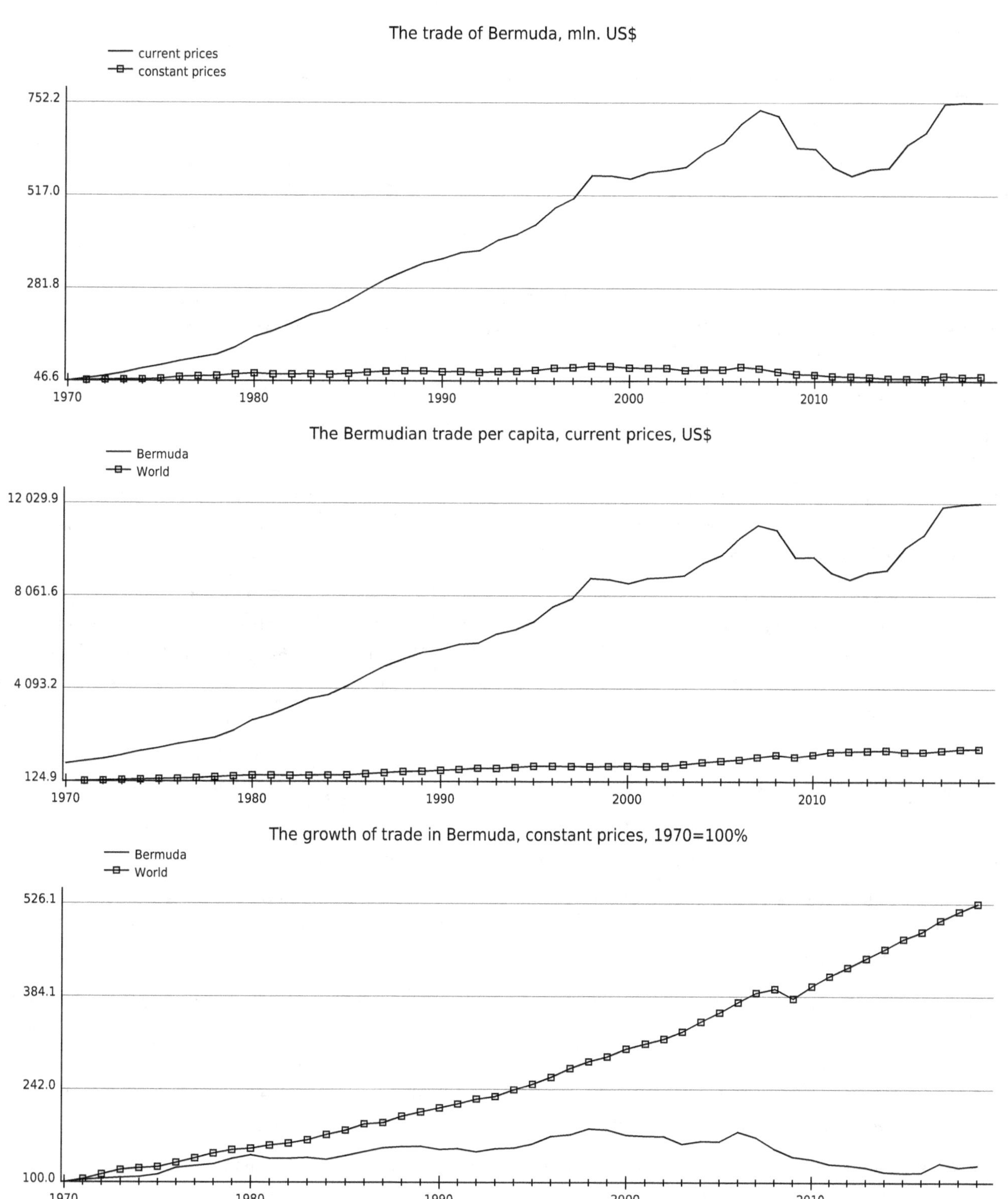

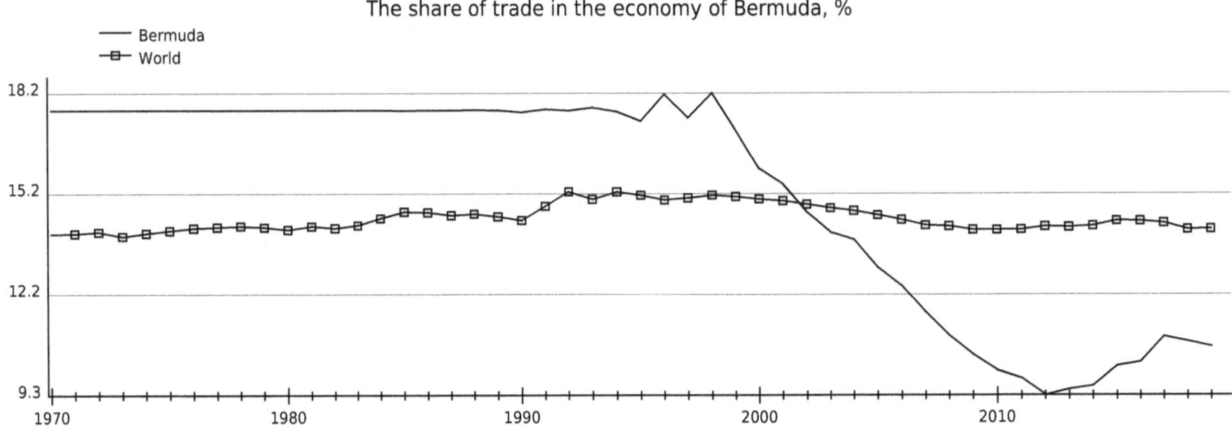

The 1970s

The trade of Bermuda was $83.7 million per year in the 1970s, ranked 129th in the world, and was on a par with Guinea-Bissau ($83.2 million), the Central African Republic ($82.1 million). The share in the world was 0.0094%, and 0.023% in the Americas.

The share of trade in the economy of Bermuda was 17.6% in the 1970s, ranked 56th in the world, and was on a par with Argentina (17.6%), Honduras (17.7%), Sudan (17.8%).

The sector of trade per capita in Bermuda was $1 521.5 in the 1970s, ranked 7th in the world. The Bermuda's trade per capita was greater than trade per capita in the world ($221.0) in 6.9 times, and was greater than trade per capita in the Americas ($654.8) in 2.3 times.

The growth of trade in Bermuda was 3.5% in the 1970s, ranked 125th in the world, and was on a par with Finland (3.4%), Bolivia (3.5%). The growth of trade in Bermuda (3.5%) was less than growth of trade in the world (4.5%), was less than growth of trade in the Americas (4.4%).

Comparison with neighbors. The Bermuda's trade was less than in the USA ($278.3 billion) and in the Bahamas ($308.5 million). The value added of trade per capita in Bermuda was greater than in the USA ($1 275.1); but less than in the Bahamas ($1 645.9). The growth of trade in Bermuda was greater than in the Bahamas (2.4%); but less than in the USA (3.9%).

Comparison with leaders. The value of trade in Bermuda was less than in the USA ($278.3 billion), in Japan ($90.3 billion), in the USSR ($62.3 billion), in Germany ($61.1 billion), and in France ($40.9 billion). The value of trade per capita in Bermuda was greater than in the United States ($1 275.1), in Japan ($811.1), in Germany ($775.5), in France ($762.4), and in the USSR ($247.1). The growth of trade in Bermuda was greater than in Germany (3.0%); but less than in Japan (8.2%), in the USSR (5.2%), in France (3.9%), and in the United States (3.9%).

The 1980s

The Bermuda's trade was $247.2 million per year in the 1980s, ranked 121st in the world. The share in the world was 0.012%, and 0.029% in the Americas.

The share of trade in the economy of Bermuda was 17.6% in the 1980s, ranked 57th in the world.

The value added of trade per capita in Bermuda was $4 160.6 in the 1980s, ranked 5th in the world. The value added of trade per capita in Bermuda was greater than trade per capita in the world ($437.7) in 9.5 times, and was greater than trade per capita in the Americas ($1 268.0) in 3.3 times.

The growth of trade in Bermuda was 1.3% in the 1980s, ranked 139th in the world, and was on a par with Brunei (1.3%). The growth of trade in Bermuda (1.3%) was less than growth of trade in the world (3.3%), was less than growth of trade in the Americas (3.5%).

Comparison with neighbors. The value of trade in Bermuda was less than in the USA ($653.3 billion) and in the Bahamas ($887.5 million). The value of trade per capita in Bermuda was greater than in the Bahamas ($3.8 thousand) and in the United States ($2.7 thousand). The growth of trade in Bermuda was less than in the Bahamas (4.5%) and in the USA (4.4%).

Comparison with leaders. The trade of Bermuda was less than in the United States ($653.3 billion), in Japan ($277.3 billion), in Germany ($116.7 billion), in the USSR ($112.3 billion), and in Italy ($95.7 billion). The trade per capita in Bermuda was greater than in the USA ($2.7 thousand), in Japan ($2.3 thousand), in Italy ($1 684.2), in Germany ($1 496.0), and in the USSR ($408.1). The growth of trade in Bermuda was greater than in the USSR (-0.62%); but less than in Japan (4.9%), in the USA (4.4%), in Italy (2.3%), and in Germany (1.8%).

The 1990s

The value added of trade in Bermuda was $449.7 million per year in the 1990s, ranked 131st in the world, and was on a par with Aruba ($446.5 million), Cambodia ($444.7 million), Burkina Faso ($443.0 million). The share in the world was 0.011%, and 0.030% in the Americas.

The share of trade in the economy of Bermuda was 17.6% in the 1990s, ranked 65th in the world, and was on a par with Melanesia (17.6%), Micronesia (17.7%), Southern Europe (17.7%).

The sector of trade per capita in Bermuda was $7 112.0 in the 1990s, ranked 5th in the world. The Bermudian trade per capita was greater than trade per capita in the world ($721.8) in 9.9 times, and was greater than trade per capita in the Americas ($1 943.2) in 3.7 times.

The growth of trade in Bermuda was 1.5% in the 1990s, ranked 142nd in the world. The growth of trade in Bermuda (1.5%) was less than growth of trade in the world (3.5%), was less than growth of trade in the Americas (3.8%).

Comparison with neighbors. The sector of trade in Bermuda was less than in the United States ($1.2 trillion) and in the Bahamas ($1.4 billion). The value of trade per capita in Bermuda was greater than in the Bahamas ($5.1 thousand) and in the United States ($4.4 thousand). The growth of trade in Bermuda was greater than in the Bahamas (0.49%); but less than in the United States (4.3%).

Comparison with leaders. The Bermudian trade was less than in the United States ($1.2 trillion), in Japan ($713.2 billion), in Germany ($243.7 billion), in Italy ($185.6 billion), and in France ($177.0 billion). The Bermuda's trade per capita was greater than in Japan ($5.7 thousand), in the USA ($4.4 thousand), in Italy ($3.3 thousand), in Germany ($3.0 thousand), and in France ($3.0 thousand). The growth of trade in Bermuda was less than in the USA (4.3%), in Japan (3.8%), in Germany (2.5%), in France (2.4%), and in Italy (1.9%).

The 2000s

The value added of trade in Bermuda was $636.7 million per year in the 2000s, ranked 142nd in the world, and was on a par with Armenia ($639.0 million), Aruba ($651.2 million). The share in the world was 0.0099%, and 0.026% in the Americas.

The share of trade in the economy of Bermuda was 12.9% in the 2000s, ranked 149th in the world, and was on a par with Colombia (12.9%), Mali (12.9%), Venezuela (12.9%).

The trade per capita in Bermuda was $9 671.1 in the 2000s, ranked 4th in the world, and was on a par with Switzerland ($9.5 thousand). The value of trade per capita in Bermuda was greater than trade per capita in the world ($990.3) in 9.8 times, and was greater than trade per capita in the Americas ($2 770.2) in 3.5 times.

The growth of trade in Bermuda was -2.5% in the 2000s, ranked 203rd in the world. The growth of trade in Bermuda (-2.5%) was less than growth of trade in the world (2.7%), was less than growth of trade in the Americas (1.6%).

Comparison with neighbors. The Bermudian trade was less than in the USA ($1.9 trillion) and in the Bahamas ($2.3 billion). The Bermudian trade per capita was greater than in the Bahamas ($7.2 thousand) and in the USA ($6.4 thousand). The growth of trade in Bermuda was less than in the Bahamas (2.1%) and in the USA (1.1%).

Comparison with leaders. The trade of Bermuda was less than in the United States ($1.9 trillion), in Japan ($771.8 billion), in Germany ($296.0 billion), in the United Kingdom ($293.5 billion), and in China ($262.0 billion). The value of trade per capita in Bermuda was greater than in the USA ($6.4 thousand), in Japan ($6.0 thousand), in the United Kingdom ($4.9 thousand), in Germany ($3.6 thousand), and in China ($197.5). The growth of trade in Bermuda was less than in China (11.9%), in Germany (1.7%), in the UK (1.3%), in the USA (1.1%), and in Japan (-0.77%).

The 2010s

The value of trade in Bermuda was $653.8 million per year in the 2010s, ranked 164th in the world, and was on a par with Fiji ($656.3 million), Djibouti ($643.3 million). The share in the world was 0.0062%, and 0.018% in the Americas.

The share of trade in the economy of Bermuda was 10.1% in the 2010s, ranked 184th in the world.

The value of trade per capita in Bermuda was $10 231.2 in the 2010s, ranked 7th in the world. The sector of trade per capita in Bermuda was greater than trade per capita in the world ($1 436.8) in 7.1 times, and was greater than trade per capita in the Americas ($3 802.7) in 2.7 times.

The growth of trade in Bermuda was -1% in the 2010s, ranked 196th in the world. The growth of trade in Bermuda (-0.97%) was less than growth of trade in the world (3.3%), was less than growth of trade in the Americas (2.1%).

Comparison with neighbors. The Bermuda's trade was 4 000.6 times lower than in the USA ($2.6 trillion) and 3.7 times lower than in the Bahamas ($2.4 billion). The sector of trade per capita in Bermuda was 25.0% higher than in the USA ($8.2 thousand) and 59.6% higher than in the Bahamas ($6.4 thousand). The growth of trade in Bermuda was less than in the United States (2.3%) and in the Bahamas (0.64%).

Comparison with leaders. The value of trade in Bermuda was 4 000.6 times lower than in the United States ($2.6 trillion), 1 826.9 times lower than in China ($1.2 trillion), 1 330.0 times lower than in Japan ($869.5 billion), 569.9 times lower than in Germany ($372.6 billion), and 504.7 times lower than in the United Kingdom ($330.0 billion). The sector of trade per capita in Bermuda was 25.0% higher than in the United States ($8.2 thousand), 50.5% higher than in Japan ($6.8 thousand), 2.0 times higher than in the UK ($5.0 thousand), 2.2 times higher than in Germany ($4.6 thousand), and 12.0 times higher than in China ($851.7). The growth of trade in Bermuda was less than in China (8.9%), in the United Kingdom (2.8%), in the United States (2.3%), in Germany (2.0%), and in Japan (0.77%).

Chapter IX. Services

(ISIC J-P)

The value of services in Bermuda increased from $303.8 million per year in the 1970s to $5.1 billion per year in the 2010s, that is by $4.8 billion or 16.8 times. The change occurred at $4.3 billion due to a 6.9-fold increase in prices, as also at $387.2 million due to a 2.1-fold increase in productivity, as well as at $49.0 million due to the growth in population. The average annual growth in services is 2.1%. The minimum value of services was in 1970 at $169.1 million. The maximum value of services was in 2019 at $5.5 billion.

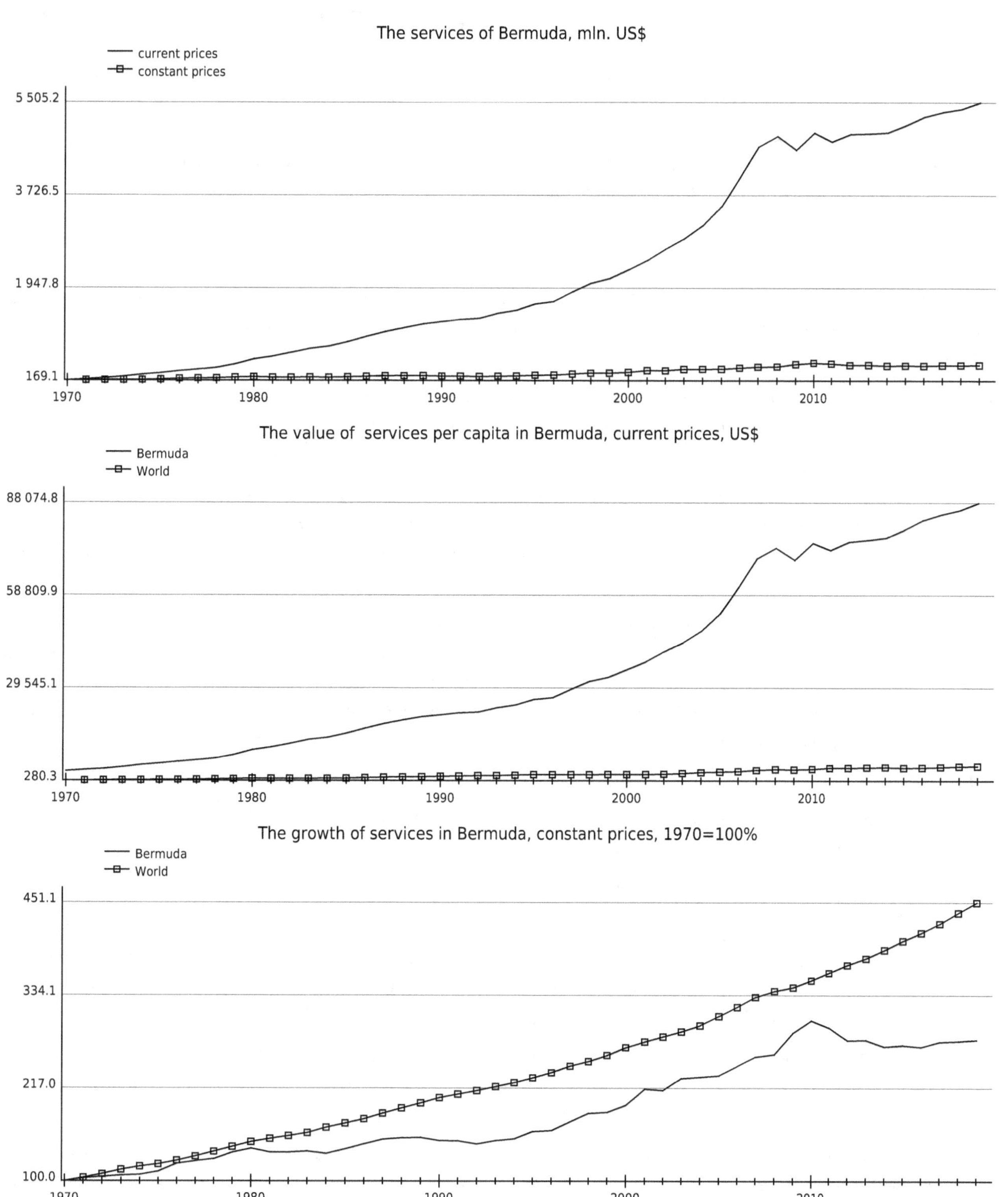

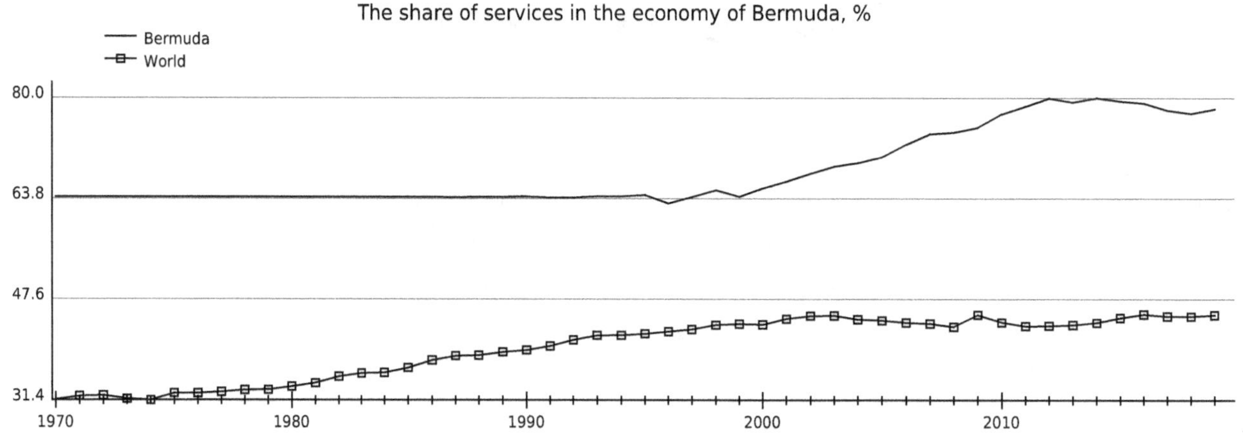

The 1970s

The value added of services in Bermuda was $303.8 million per year in the 1970s, ranked 108th in the world, and was on a par with Namibia ($301.4 million). The share in the world was 0.015%, and 0.036% in the Americas.

The share of services in the economy of Bermuda was 64.0% in the 1970s, ranked 3rd in the world, and was on a par with Macao (64.2%).

The sector of services per capita in Bermuda was $5 520.7 in the 1970s, ranked 2nd in the world. The sector of services per capita in Bermuda was greater than services per capita in the world ($506.9) in 10.9 times, and was greater than services per capita in the Americas ($1 502.8) in 3.7 times.

The growth of services in Bermuda was 3.5% in the 1970s, ranked 136th in the world, and was on a par with Zimbabwe (3.4%). The growth of services in Bermuda (3.5%) was less than growth of services in the world (4.1%), was less than growth of services in the Americas (3.7%).

Comparison with neighbors. The value added of services in Bermuda was less than in the United States ($674.4 billion) and in the Bahamas ($484.4 million). The sector of services per capita in Bermuda was greater than in the United States ($3.1 thousand) and in the Bahamas ($2.6 thousand). The growth of services in Bermuda was greater than in the United States (3.3%) and in the Bahamas (2.4%).

Comparison with leaders. The value of services in Bermuda was less than in the United States ($674.4 billion), in the USSR ($168.3 billion), in Japan ($153.8 billion), in Germany ($150.2 billion), and in France ($121.8 billion). The value of services per capita in Bermuda was greater than in the USA ($3.1 thousand), in France ($2.3 thousand), in Germany ($1 907.6), in Japan ($1 381.3), and in the USSR ($667.3). The growth of services in Bermuda was greater than in the USA (3.3%) and in the USSR (0.90%); but less than in Japan (5.9%), in Germany (4.8%), and in France (3.9%).

The 1980s

The services of Bermuda were $896.7 million per year in the 1980s, ranked 104th in the world, and were on a par with DR Congo ($907.1 million), Macao ($882.0 million). The share in the world was 0.017%, and 0.039% in the Americas.

The share of services in the economy of Bermuda was 64.0% in the 1980s, ranked 3rd in the world, and was on a par with Macao (64.4%).

The value of services per capita in Bermuda was $15 094.5 in the 1980s, ranked 3rd in the world. The value added of services per capita in Bermuda was greater than services per capita in the world ($1 115.5) in 13.5 times, and was greater than services per capita in the Americas ($3 456.8) in 4.4 times.

The growth of services in Bermuda was 1.3% in the 1980s, ranked 157th in the world, and was on a par with Denmark (1.3%). The growth of services in Bermuda (1.3%) was less than growth of services in the world (3.3%), was less than growth of services in the Americas (2.8%).

Comparison with neighbors. The services of Bermuda were less than in the United States ($1.9 trillion) and in the Bahamas ($1.4 billion). The Bermuda's services per capita were greater than in the USA ($7.8 thousand) and in the Bahamas ($6.0 thousand). The growth of services in Bermuda was less than in the Bahamas (3.4%) and in the United States (2.8%).

Comparison with leaders. The value added of services in Bermuda was less than in the USA ($1.9 trillion), in Japan ($619.9 billion), in Germany ($362.2 billion), in France ($294.5 billion), and in the UK ($265.4 billion). The services per capita in Bermuda were greater than in the USA ($7.8 thousand), in France ($5.2 thousand), in Japan ($5.1 thousand), in the UK ($4.7 thousand), and in Germany ($4.6 thousand). The growth of services in Bermuda was less than in Japan (4.8%), in the United Kingdom (3.3%), in Germany (3.1%), in the USA (2.8%), and in France (2.3%).

The 1990s

The services of Bermuda were $1.6 billion per year in the 1990s, ranked 105th in the world, and were on a par with Iraq ($1.7 billion). The share in the world was 0.014%, and 0.034% in the Americas.

The share of services in the economy of Bermuda was 64.1% in the 1990s, ranked 3rd in the world.

The value of services per capita in Bermuda was $25 870.3 in the 1990s, ranked 4th in the world. The sector of services per capita in Bermuda was greater than services per capita in the world ($2 014.6) in 12.8 times, and was greater than services per capita in the Americas ($6 173.1) in 4.2 times.

The growth of services in Bermuda was 1.9% in the 1990s, ranked 141st in the world, and was on a par with French Polynesia (1.9%). The growth of services in Bermuda (1.9%) was less than growth of services in the world (2.7%), was less than growth of services in the Americas (2.4%).

Comparison with neighbors. The services of Bermuda were less than in the United States ($3.8 trillion) and in the Bahamas ($2.8 billion). The Bermuda's services per capita were greater than in the USA ($14.4 thousand) and in the Bahamas ($10.0 thousand). The growth of services in Bermuda was less than in the Bahamas (3.1%) and in the United States (2.3%).

Comparison with leaders. The value of services in Bermuda was less than in the United States ($3.8 trillion), in Japan ($1.6 trillion), in Germany ($908.0 billion), in France ($628.2 billion), and in the United Kingdom ($592.3 billion). The sector of services per capita in Bermuda was greater than in the USA ($14.4 thousand), in Japan ($12.8 thousand), in Germany ($11.3 thousand), in France ($10.6 thousand), and in the UK ($10.2 thousand). The growth of services in Bermuda was greater than in Japan (1.7%) and in France (1.6%); but less than in Germany (3.2%), in the UK (3.0%), and in the United States (2.3%).

The 2000s

The value of services in Bermuda was $3.5 billion per year in the 2000s, ranked 103rd in the world, and was on a par with Ghana ($3.5 billion), Trinidad and Tobago ($3.6 billion), Yemen ($3.6 billion). The share in the world was 0.018%, and 0.043% in the Americas.

The share of services in the economy of Bermuda was 71.2% in the 2000s, ranked 2nd in the world.

The sector of services per capita in Bermuda was $53 426.0 in the 2000s, ranked 1st in the world, and was on a par with the Cayman Islands ($53.4 thousand). The sector of services per capita in Bermuda was greater than services per capita in the world ($3 011.2) in 17.7 times, and was greater than services per capita in the Americas ($9 407.5) in 5.7 times.

The growth of services in Bermuda was 4.4% in the 2000s, ranked 82nd in the world, and was on a par with Panama (4.3%), Saudi Arabia (4.4%), Spain (4.4%). The growth of services in Bermuda (4.4%) was greater than growth of services in the world (2.9%), was greater than growth of services in the Americas (2.2%).

Comparison with neighbors. The Bermuda's services were less than in the United States ($6.7 trillion) and in the Bahamas ($4.7 billion). The sector of services per capita in Bermuda was greater than in the United States ($22.9 thousand) and in the Bahamas ($14.4 thousand). The growth of services in Bermuda was greater than in the USA (2.0%) and in the Bahamas (-0.063%).

Comparison with leaders. The services of Bermuda were less than in the United States ($6.7 trillion), in Japan ($2.0 trillion), in Germany ($1.2 trillion), in the UK ($1.1 trillion), and in France ($997.0 billion). The services per capita in Bermuda were greater than in the USA ($22.9 thousand), in the United Kingdom ($18.0 thousand), in France ($15.9 thousand), in Japan ($15.3 thousand), and in Germany ($15.0 thousand). The growth of services in Bermuda was greater than in the United Kingdom (2.7%), in the United States (2.0%), in France (1.5%), in Japan (1.2%), and in Germany (0.57%).

The 2010s

The value added of services in Bermuda was $5.1 billion per year in the 2010s, ranked 121st in the world, and was on a par with DPRK

($5.1 billion), Jamaica ($5.2 billion). The share in the world was 0.016%, and 0.040% in the Americas.

The share of services in the economy of Bermuda was 78.7% in the 2010s, ranked 1st in the world.

The services per capita in Bermuda were $79 656.4 in the 2010s, ranked 2nd in the world. The services per capita in Bermuda were greater than services per capita in the world ($4 467.8) in 17.8 times, and were greater than services per capita in the Americas ($13 184.6) in 6.0 times.

The growth of services in Bermuda was -0.3% in the 2010s, ranked 196th in the world. The growth of services in Bermuda (-0.30%) was less than growth of services in the world (2.7%), was less than growth of services in the Americas (1.8%).

Comparison with neighbors. The value added of services in Bermuda was 1 955.8 times lower than in the United States ($10.0 trillion) and 7.7% lower than in the Bahamas ($5.5 billion). The Bermudian services per capita were 2.6 times higher than in the United States ($31.2 thousand) and 5.4 times higher than in the Bahamas ($14.8 thousand). The growth of services in Bermuda was less than in the United States (1.8%) and in the Bahamas (1.3%).

Comparison with leaders. The value added of services in Bermuda was 1 955.8 times lower than in the USA ($10.0 trillion), 696.9 times lower than in China ($3.5 trillion), 446.7 times lower than in Japan ($2.3 trillion), 315.8 times lower than in Germany ($1.6 trillion), and 266.3 times lower than in the UK ($1.4 trillion). The value added of services per capita in Bermuda was 2.6 times higher than in the United States ($31.2 thousand), 3.9 times higher than in the United Kingdom ($20.7 thousand), 4.1 times higher than in Germany ($19.6 thousand), 4.5 times higher than in Japan ($17.8 thousand), and 31.5 times higher than in China ($2.5 thousand). The growth of services in Bermuda was less than in China (8.4%), in the USA (1.8%), in the UK (1.7%), in Germany (1.2%), and in Japan (0.99%).

Part III. External relations

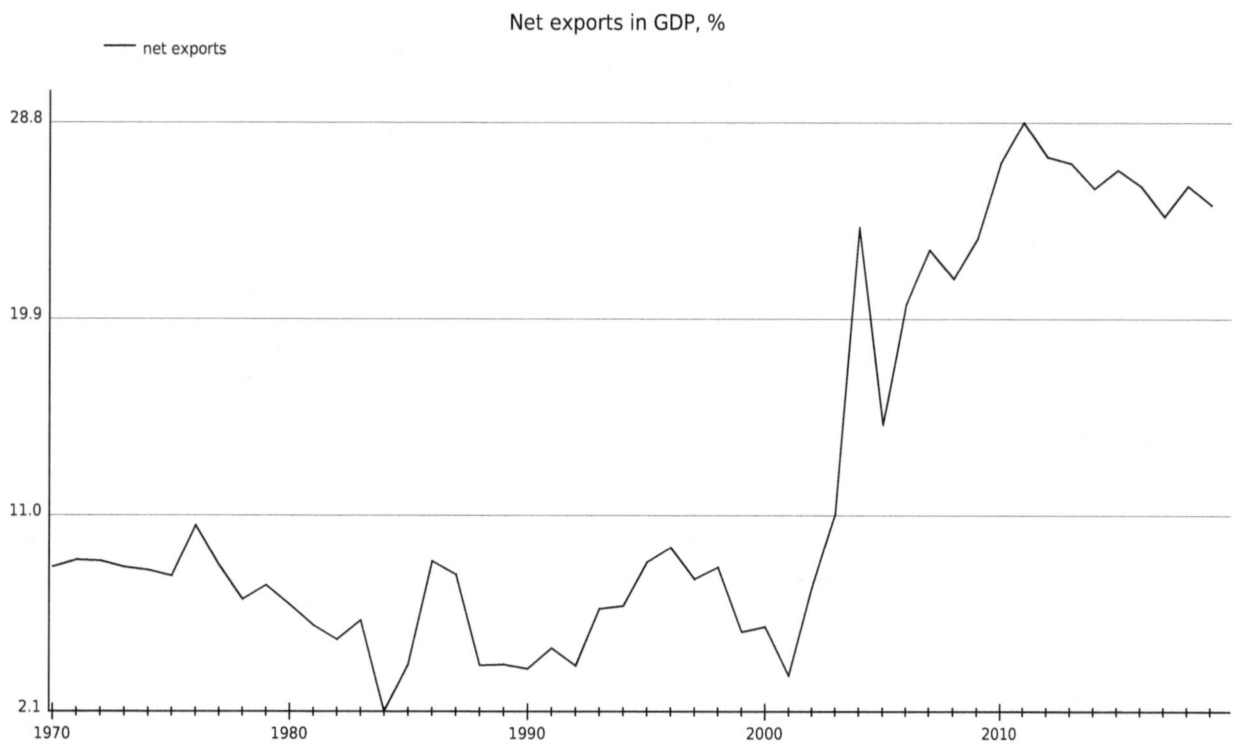

Chapter X. Exports

Exports of goods and services

The Bermuda's exports grew up from $244.0 million per year in the 1970s to $3.4 billion per year in the 2010s, that is by $3.2 billion or 14.0 times. The change occurred at $2.9 billion due to a 6.9-fold increase in prices, as also at $214.6 million due to a 1.8-fold increase in per capita rate, as well as at $39.4 million due to the rise in population. The average annual growth in exports is 1.8%. The minimum value of exports was in 1970 at $136.1 million. The maximum value of exports was in 2019 at $3.8 billion.

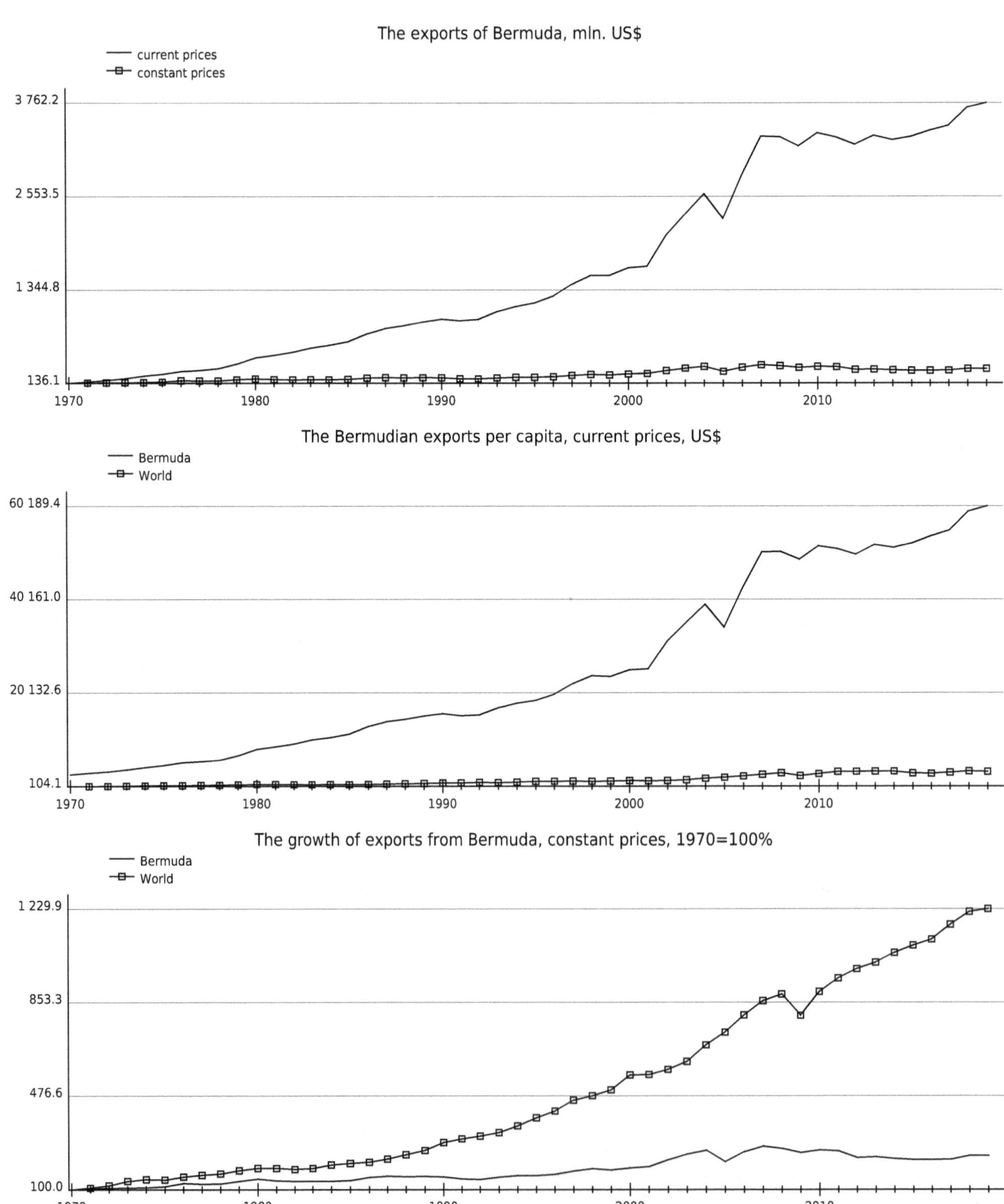

The exports of Bermuda, mln. US$

The Bermudian exports per capita, current prices, US$

The growth of exports from Bermuda, constant prices, 1970=100%

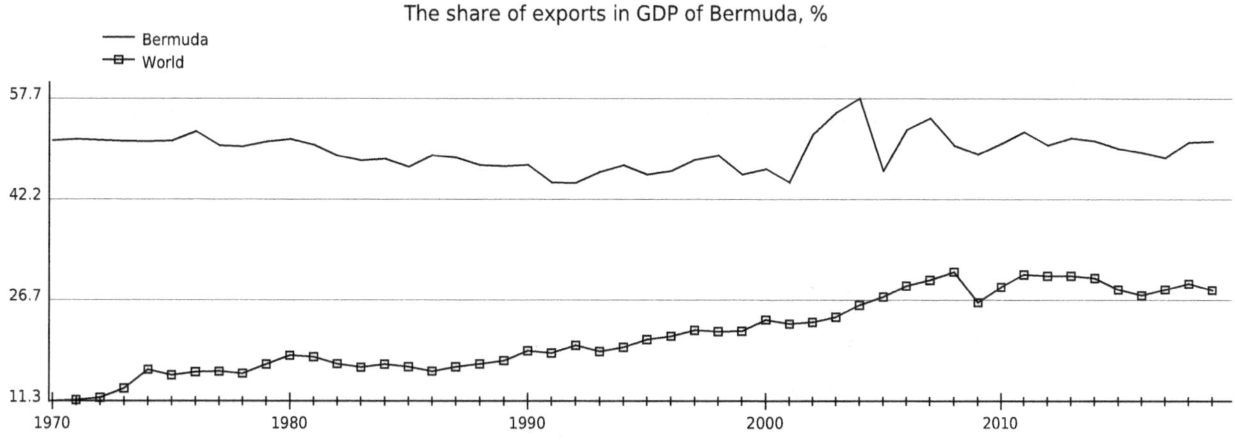

The 1970s

The Bermuda's exports were $244.0 million per year in the 1970s, ranked 116th in the world, and were on a par with Benin ($242.0 million), Togo ($239.0 million). The share in the world was 0.025%, and 0.11% from the Americas.

The share of exports in GDP of Bermuda was 51.2% in the 1970s, ranked 36th in the world, and was on a par with Saint Lucia (51.0%), the Virgin Islands (50.9%).

The exports per capita from Bermuda were $4 434.6 in the 1970s, ranked 10th in the world, and were on a par with the Bahamas ($4.4 thousand). The value of exports per capita from Bermuda was greater than exports per capita in the world ($242.1) in 18.3 times, and was greater than exports per capita from the Americas ($397.2) in 11.2 times.

The growth of exports from Bermuda was 3.3% in the 1970s, ranked 132nd in the world. The growth of exports from Bermuda (3.3%) was less than growth of exports in the world (6.5%), was less than growth of exports from the Americas (6.4%).

Comparison with neighbors. The Bermudian exports were less than from the USA ($128.0 billion) and from the Bahamas ($826.0 million). The Bermuda's exports per capita were greater than from the Bahamas ($4.4 thousand) and from the USA ($586.5). The growth of exports from Bermuda was greater than from the Bahamas (0.34%); but less than from the United States (6.8%).

Comparison with leaders. The value of exports from Bermuda was less than from the USA ($128.0 billion), from Germany ($82.9 billion), from France ($64.3 billion), from Japan ($64.1 billion), and from the United Kingdom ($61.3 billion). The exports per capita from Bermuda were greater than from France ($1 199.1), from the UK ($1 094.1), from Germany ($1 052.2), from the United States ($586.5), and from Japan ($575.8). The growth of exports from Bermuda was less than from Japan (8.6%), from France (7.8%), from the United States (6.8%), from Germany (5.1%), and from the UK (5.0%).

The 1980s

The exports of Bermuda were $682.2 million per year in the 1980s, ranked 106th in the world. The share in the world was 0.027%, and 0.12% from the Americas.

The share of exports in GDP of Bermuda was 48.5% in the 1980s, ranked 38th in the world, and was on a par with the Caribbean (48.0%).

The exports per capita from Bermuda were $11 483.5 in the 1980s, ranked 8th in the world. The value of exports per capita from Bermuda was greater than exports per capita in the world ($529.9) in 21.7 times, and was greater than exports per capita from the Americas ($890.9) in 12.9 times.

The growth of exports from Bermuda was 1.4% in the 1980s, ranked 135th in the world, and was on a par with South Africa (1.4%). The growth of exports from Bermuda (1.4%) was less than growth of exports in the world (3.8%), was less than growth of exports from the Americas (5.1%).

Comparison with neighbors. The exports of Bermuda were less than from the United States ($338.6 billion) and from the Bahamas ($2.3 billion). The value of exports per capita from Bermuda was greater than from the Bahamas ($9.7 thousand) and from the United States ($1 413.8). The growth of exports from Bermuda was greater than from the Bahamas (0.64%); but less than from the USA (5.7%).

Comparison with leaders. The Bermuda's exports were less than from the United States ($338.6 billion), from Japan ($210.6 billion), from Germany ($208.1 billion), from France ($155.9 billion), and from the UK ($155.0 billion). The exports per capita from Bermuda were greater than from France ($2.8 thousand), from the UK ($2.7 thousand), from Germany ($2.7 thousand), from Japan ($1 736.5), and from the United States ($1 413.8). The growth of exports from Bermuda was less than from Japan (6.7%), from the United States (5.7%), from Germany (4.7%), from France (4.0%), and from the United Kingdom (3.0%).

The 1990s

The value of exports from Bermuda was $1.2 billion per year in the 1990s, ranked 119th in the world, and was on a par with the Cayman Islands ($1.2 billion), Zambia ($1.2 billion). The share in the world was 0.020%, and 0.093% from the Americas.

The share of exports in GDP of Bermuda was 46.8% in the 1990s, ranked 55th in the world, and was on a par with Kuwait (47.1%).

The Bermuda's exports per capita were $18 952.6 in the 1990s, ranked 9th in the world. The value of exports per capita from Bermuda was greater than exports per capita in the world ($1 029.5) in 18.4 times, and was greater than exports per capita from the Americas ($1 662.5) in 11.4 times.

The growth of exports from Bermuda was 1.6% in the 1990s, ranked 157th in the world, and was on a par with Niger (1.5%), Mauritania (1.6%). The growth of exports from Bermuda (1.6%) was less than growth of exports in the world (6.9%), was less than growth of exports from the Americas (7.3%).

Comparison with neighbors. The Bermudian exports were less than from the USA ($773.6 billion) and from the Bahamas ($2.3 billion). The exports per capita from Bermuda were greater than from the Bahamas ($8.2 thousand) and from the USA ($2.9 thousand). The growth of exports from Bermuda was greater than from the Bahamas (0.82%); but less than from the USA (7.2%).

Comparison with leaders. The exports of Bermuda were less than from the USA ($773.6 billion), from Germany ($509.0 billion), from Japan ($418.7 billion), from France ($329.8 billion), and from the United Kingdom ($324.3 billion). The exports per capita from Bermuda were greater than from Germany ($6.3 thousand), from the United Kingdom ($5.6 thousand), from France ($5.6 thousand), from Japan ($3.3 thousand), and from the USA ($2.9 thousand). The growth of exports from Bermuda was less than from the USA (7.2%), from France (6.5%), from Germany (6.0%), from the UK (5.7%), and from Japan (4.2%).

The 2000s

The value of exports from Bermuda was $2.5 billion per year in the 2000s, ranked 124th in the world, and was on a par with the Cayman Islands ($2.5 billion). The share in the world was 0.020%, and 0.10% from the Americas.

The structure of exports: primary products (7.0%), resource-based manufactures (7.7%), low technology manufactures (9.3%), medium technology manufactures (48.9%), and high technology manufactures (21.8%).

Bermuda exported goods to France (54.1%), Norway (8.4%), Spain (7.6%), the USA (3.7%), Brazil (3.1%) and other countries (23.1%).

The share of exports in GDP of Bermuda was 51.2% in the 2000s, ranked 58th in the world, and was on a par with the Caribbean (51.2%), Guyana (51.1%).

The exports per capita from Bermuda were $38 270.2 in the 2000s, ranked 9th in the world. The value of exports per capita from Bermuda was greater than exports per capita in the world ($1 933.7) in 19.8 times, and was greater than exports per capita from the Americas ($2 781.7) in 13.8 times.

The growth of exports from Bermuda was 3.4% in the 2000s, ranked 129th in the world, and was on a par with Palestine (3.4%), Kiribati (3.4%). The growth of exports from Bermuda (3.4%) was less than growth of exports in the world (4.8%), was greater than growth of exports from the Americas (2.9%).

Comparison with neighbors. The Bermudian exports were less than from the United States ($1.3 trillion) and from the Bahamas ($3.5 billion). The Bermuda's exports per capita were greater than from the Bahamas ($10.9 thousand) and from the United States ($4.5 thousand). The growth of exports from Bermuda was greater than from the United States (3.3%) and from the Bahamas (1.5%).

Comparison with leaders. The Bermuda's exports were less than from the USA ($1.3 trillion), from Germany ($1.0 trillion), from China ($780.2 billion), from Japan ($626.3 billion), and from the UK ($591.1 billion). The value of exports per capita from Bermuda was greater than from Germany ($12.8 thousand), from the United Kingdom ($9.8 thousand), from Japan ($4.9 thousand), from the USA ($4.5 thousand), and from China ($588.1). The growth of exports from Bermuda was greater than from the USA (3.3%) and from the

UK (2.8%); but less than from China (12.7%), from Germany (5.0%), and from Japan (3.5%).

The 2010s

The exports of Bermuda were $3.4 billion per year in the 2010s, ranked 138th in the world, and were on a par with Burkina Faso ($3.5 billion), Mali ($3.4 billion). The share in the world was 0.015%, and 0.084% from the Americas.

The structure of exports: primary products (19.3%), resource-based manufactures (7.1%), low technology manufactures (1.5%), medium technology manufactures (39.1%), and high technology manufactures (17.0%).

Bermuda exported goods to the USA (14.5%), Spain (13.1%), Indonesia (11.2%), Germany (8.0%), Cyprus (7.9%) and other countries (45.3%).

The share of exports in GDP of Bermuda was 50.6% in the 2010s, ranked 60th in the world, and was on a par with Macedonia (50.6%), Suriname (50.7%).

The Bermudian exports per capita were $53 504.9 in the 2010s, ranked 9th in the world. The value of exports per capita from Bermuda was greater than exports per capita in the world ($3 098.9) in 17.3 times, and was greater than exports per capita from the Americas ($4 197.2) in 12.7 times.

The growth of exports from Bermuda was -0.5% in the 2010s, ranked 190th in the world. The growth of exports from Bermuda (-0.50%) was less than growth of exports in the world (4.4%), was less than growth of exports from the Americas (3.6%).

Comparison with neighbors. The value of exports from Bermuda was 663.9 times lower than from the USA ($2.3 trillion) and 21.7% lower than from the Bahamas ($4.4 billion). The exports per capita from Bermuda were 4.6 times higher than from the Bahamas ($11.7 thousand) and 7.5 times higher than from the United States ($7.1 thousand). The growth of exports from Bermuda was less than from the USA (3.7%) and from the Bahamas (3.0%).

Comparison with leaders. The exports of Bermuda were 670.8 times lower than from China ($2.3 trillion), 663.9 times lower than from the USA ($2.3 trillion), 492.3 times lower than from Germany ($1.7 trillion), 251.4 times lower than from Japan ($859.4 billion), and 238.4 times lower than from the UK ($815.1 billion). The exports per capita from Bermuda were 2.6 times higher than from Germany ($20.6 thousand), 4.3 times higher than from the United Kingdom ($12.4 thousand), 7.5 times higher than from the USA ($7.1 thousand), 8.0 times higher than from Japan ($6.7 thousand), and 32.7 times higher than from China ($1 635.3). The growth of exports from Bermuda was less than from China (6.8%), from Germany (4.7%), from Japan (4.6%), from the USA (3.7%), and from the UK (3.1%).

Chapter XI. Imports

Imports of goods and services

The imports of Bermuda grew up from $203.4 million per year in the 1970s to $1.6 billion per year in the 2010s, that is by $1.4 billion or 8.1 times. The change occurred at $1.3 billion due to a 4.8-fold increase in prices, as also at $102.0 million due to a 1.4-fold increase in per capita rate, as well as at $32.8 million due to the increase in population. The average annual growth in imports is 1.5%. The minimum value of imports was in 1970 at $113.2 million. The maximum value of imports was in 2007 at $1.9 billion.

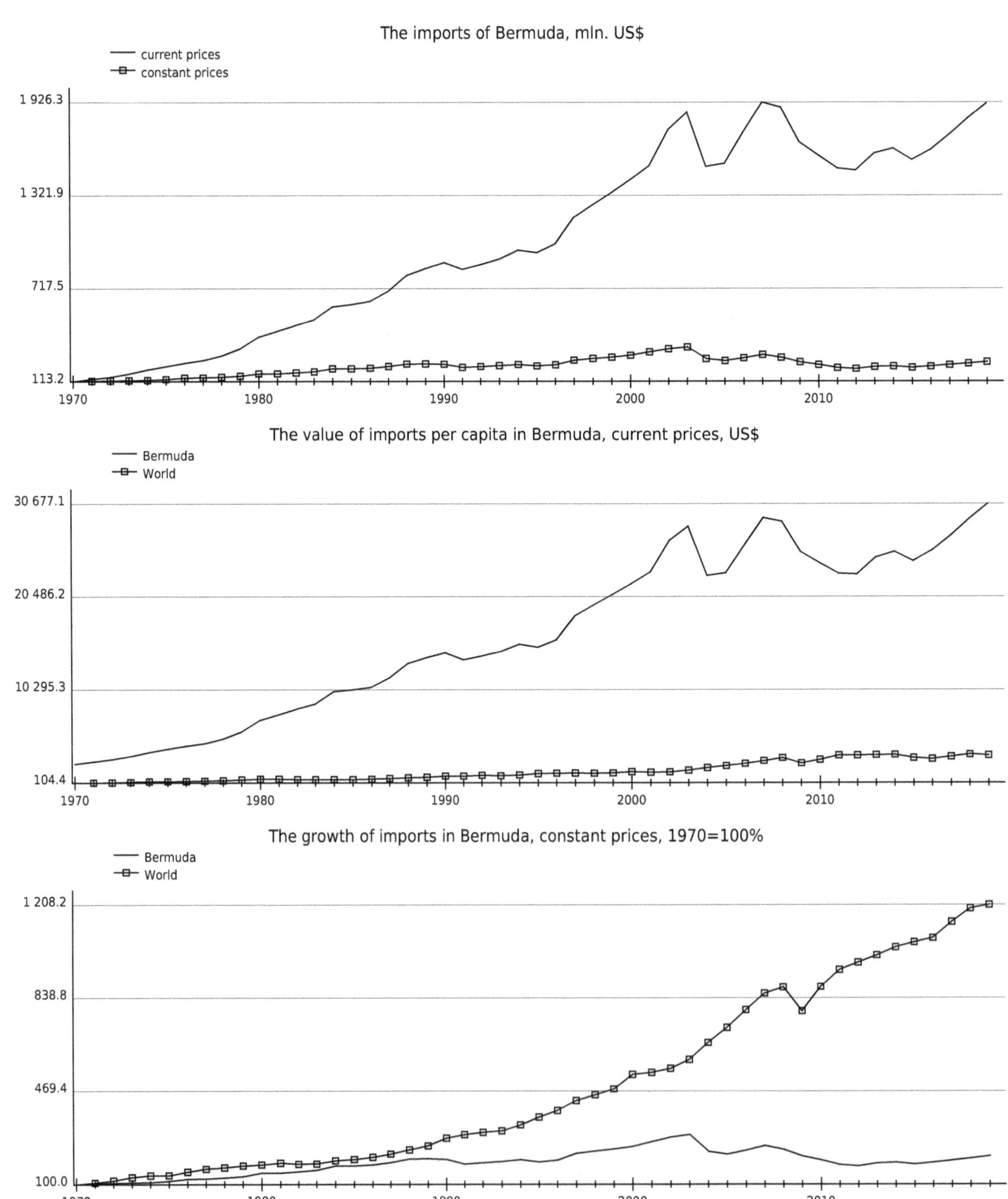

The imports of Bermuda, mln. US$

The value of imports per capita in Bermuda, current prices, US$

The growth of imports in Bermuda, constant prices, 1970=100%

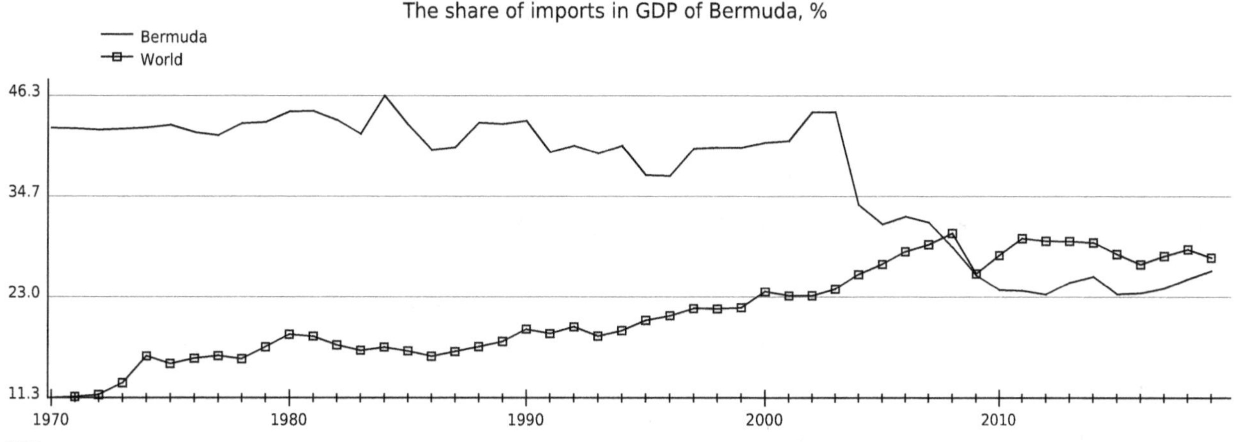

The 1970s

The value of imports in Bermuda was $203.4 million per year in the 1970s, ranked 137th in the world, and was on a par with the CAR ($199.0 million). The share in the world was 0.021%, and 0.086% in the Americas.

The share of imports in GDP of Bermuda was 42.6% in the 1970s, ranked 66th in the world, and was on a par with Melanesia (42.2%).

The imports per capita in Bermuda were $3 695.8 in the 1970s, ranked 12th in the world, and were on a par with Aruba ($3.6 thousand). The Bermudian imports per capita were greater than imports per capita in the world ($244.3) in 15.1 times, and were greater than imports per capita in the Americas ($421.7) in 8.8 times.

The growth of imports in Bermuda was 3% in the 1970s, ranked 149th in the world. The growth of imports in Bermuda (3.0%) was less than growth of imports in the world (6.3%), was less than growth of imports in the Americas (5.4%).

Comparison with neighbors. The imports of Bermuda were less than in the United States ($133.2 billion) and in the Bahamas ($635.1 million). The imports per capita in Bermuda were greater than in the Bahamas ($3.4 thousand) and in the United States ($610.4). The growth of imports in Bermuda was greater than in the Bahamas (0.64%); but less than in the United States (5.1%).

Comparison with leaders. The Bermuda's imports were less than in the United States ($133.2 billion), in Germany ($92.5 billion), in France ($63.3 billion), in the United Kingdom ($62.4 billion), and in Japan ($61.0 billion). The imports per capita in Bermuda were greater than in France ($1 181.1), in Germany ($1 175.1), in the United Kingdom ($1 113.2), in the United States ($610.4), and in Japan ($547.6). The growth of imports in Bermuda was less than in France (7.2%), in Japan (7.0%), in Germany (5.6%), in the United States (5.1%), and in the UK (4.5%).

The 1980s

The Bermuda's imports were $603.1 million per year in the 1980s, ranked 120th in the world, and were on a par with Niger ($598.5 million), Nepal ($596.4 million), Greenland ($591.2 million). The share in the world was 0.023%, and 0.092% in the Americas.

The share of imports in GDP of Bermuda was 42.8% in the 1980s, ranked 72nd in the world, and was on a par with Trinidad and Tobago (42.6%).

The value of imports per capita in Bermuda was $10 151.8 in the 1980s, ranked 8th in the world. The value of imports per capita in Bermuda was greater than imports per capita in the world ($539.1) in 18.8 times, and was greater than imports per capita in the Americas ($984.9) in 10.3 times.

The growth of imports in Bermuda was 4.4% in the 1980s, ranked 57th in the world. The growth of imports in Bermuda (4.4%) was greater than growth of imports in the world (3.8%), was greater than growth of imports in the Americas (3.8%).

Comparison with neighbors. The Bermuda's imports were less than in the USA ($417.2 billion) and in the Bahamas ($1.8 billion). The value of imports per capita in Bermuda was greater than in the Bahamas ($7.8 thousand) and in the USA ($1 742.4). The growth of imports in Bermuda was greater than in the Bahamas (4.3%); but less than in the United States (5.8%).

Comparison with leaders. The Bermudian imports were less than in the United States ($417.2 billion), in Germany ($225.6 billion), in Japan ($175.9 billion), in France ($162.0 billion), and in the UK ($157.7 billion). The imports per capita in Bermuda were greater than in Germany ($2.9 thousand), in France ($2.9 thousand), in the United Kingdom ($2.8 thousand), in the USA ($1 742.4), and in Japan

($1 450.4). The growth of imports in Bermuda was greater than in France (4.3%) and in Germany (3.3%); but less than in the USA (5.8%), in the United Kingdom (5.1%), and in Japan (4.6%).

The 1990s

The value of imports in Bermuda was $1.0 billion per year in the 1990s, ranked 140th in the world, and was on a par with Fiji ($1.0 billion), Barbados ($1.0 billion). The share in the world was 0.018%, and 0.073% in the Americas.

The share of imports in GDP of Bermuda was 39.8% in the 1990s, ranked 101st in the world, and was on a par with Croatia (39.8%), the Comoros (39.9%).

The value of imports per capita in Bermuda was $16 140.2 in the 1990s, ranked 10th in the world. The value of imports per capita in Bermuda was greater than imports per capita in the world ($1 015.5) in 15.9 times, and was greater than imports per capita in the Americas ($1 812.7) in 8.9 times.

The growth of imports in Bermuda was 1.7% in the 1990s, ranked 151st in the world. The growth of imports in Bermuda (1.7%) was less than growth of imports in the world (6.6%), was less than growth of imports in the Americas (8.2%).

Comparison with neighbors. The value of imports in Bermuda was less than in the USA ($874.1 billion) and in the Bahamas ($2.3 billion). The Bermuda's imports per capita were greater than in the Bahamas ($8.3 thousand) and in the United States ($3.3 thousand). The growth of imports in Bermuda was less than in the USA (8.3%) and in the Bahamas (4.3%).

Comparison with leaders. The Bermuda's imports were less than in the USA ($874.1 billion), in Germany ($501.6 billion), in Japan ($355.9 billion), in the UK ($330.2 billion), and in France ($308.5 billion). The Bermudian imports per capita were greater than in Germany ($6.2 thousand), in the United Kingdom ($5.7 thousand), in France ($5.2 thousand), in the United States ($3.3 thousand), and in Japan ($2.8 thousand). The growth of imports in Bermuda was less than in the United States (8.3%), in Germany (6.4%), in France (5.1%), in the UK (5.1%), and in Japan (3.3%).

The 2000s

The imports of Bermuda were $1.7 billion per year in the 2000s, ranked 154th in the world, and were on a par with Fiji ($1.7 billion). The share in the world was 0.014%, and 0.057% in the Americas.

The structure of imports: primary products (18.1%), resource-based manufactures (8.4%), low technology manufactures (6.0%), medium technology manufactures (46.7%), and high technology manufactures (14.7%).

Bermuda imported goods from Kazakhstan (19.2%), South Korea (17.5%), the United States (15.9%), Italy (10.5%), Germany (5.3%) and other countries (31.5%).

The share of imports in GDP of Bermuda was 34.2% in the 2000s, ranked 137th in the world, and was on a par with Yemen (34.1%), Oman (34.1%), Malawi (34.3%).

The value of imports per capita in Bermuda was $25 524.1 in the 2000s, ranked 12th in the world. The value of imports per capita in Bermuda was greater than imports per capita in the world ($1 899.9) in 13.4 times, and was greater than imports per capita in the Americas ($3 354.4) in 7.6 times.

The growth of imports in Bermuda was -1.2% in the 2000s, ranked 203rd in the world. The growth of imports in Bermuda (-1.2%) was less than growth of imports in the world (5.1%), was less than growth of imports in the Americas (3.5%).

Comparison with neighbors. The imports of Bermuda were less than in the USA ($1.9 trillion) and in the Bahamas ($4.0 billion). The value of imports per capita in Bermuda was greater than in the Bahamas ($12.3 thousand) and in the USA ($6.4 thousand). The growth of imports in Bermuda was less than in the USA (2.8%) and in the Bahamas (0.45%).

Comparison with leaders. The Bermuda's imports were less than in the United States ($1.9 trillion), in Germany ($914.7 billion), in the UK ($641.8 billion), in China ($641.1 billion), and in Japan ($566.4 billion). The value of imports per capita in Bermuda was greater than in Germany ($11.2 thousand), in the UK ($10.6 thousand), in the USA ($6.4 thousand), in Japan ($4.4 thousand), and in China ($483.3). The growth of imports in Bermuda was less than in China (15.1%), in Germany (3.7%), in the United Kingdom (3.1%), in the United States (2.8%), and in Japan (1.8%).

The 2010s

The imports of Bermuda were $1.6 billion per year in the 2010s, ranked 173rd in the world. The share in the world was 0.0074%, and

0.034% in the Americas.

The structure of imports: primary products (3.2%), resource-based manufactures (10.9%), low technology manufactures (5.0%), medium technology manufactures (62.3%), and high technology manufactures (5.5%).

Bermuda imported goods from Republic of Korea (46.0%), the United States (20.0%), China (7.8%), Germany (7.5%), Singapore (3.8%) and other countries (14.9%).

The share of imports in GDP of Bermuda was 24.3% in the 2010s, ranked 190th in the world, and was on a par with Egypt (24.4%).

The imports per capita in Bermuda were $25 668.6 in the 2010s, ranked 20th in the world, and were on a par with Iceland ($25.3 thousand), Macao ($26.1 thousand). The Bermudian imports per capita were greater than imports per capita in the world ($3 015.6) in 8.5 times, and were greater than imports per capita in the Americas ($4 884.3) in 5.3 times.

The growth of imports in Bermuda was 0% in the 2010s, ranked 189th in the world. The growth of imports in Bermuda (0.019%) was less than growth of imports in the world (4.4%), was less than growth of imports in the Americas (3.3%).

Comparison with neighbors. The Bermudian imports were 1 717.6 times lower than in the USA ($2.8 trillion) and 3.0 times lower than in the Bahamas ($4.9 billion). The value of imports per capita in Bermuda was 97.1% higher than in the Bahamas ($13.0 thousand) and 2.9 times higher than in the United States ($8.8 thousand). The growth of imports in Bermuda was less than in the USA (4.4%) and in the Bahamas (1.6%).

Comparison with leaders. The imports of Bermuda were 1 717.6 times lower than in the USA ($2.8 trillion), 1 261.5 times lower than in China ($2.1 trillion), 886.9 times lower than in Germany ($1.5 trillion), 535.3 times lower than in Japan ($877.9 billion), and 521.1 times lower than in the United Kingdom ($854.8 billion). The imports per capita in Bermuda were 44.4% higher than in Germany ($17.8 thousand), 97.0% higher than in the UK ($13.0 thousand), 2.9 times higher than in the USA ($8.8 thousand), 3.7 times higher than in Japan ($6.9 thousand), and 17.4 times higher than in China ($1 475.4). The growth of imports in Bermuda was less than in China (8.2%), in Germany (4.8%), in the USA (4.4%), in Japan (3.8%), and in the UK (3.6%).

Part IV. Consumption

Chapter XII. Government consumption expenditure

General government final consumption expenditure

The Bermuda's government expenditure grew from $46.7 million per year in the 1970s to $863.3 million per year in the 2010s, that is by $816.6 million or 18.5 times. The change occurred at $748.7 million due to a 7.5-fold increase in prices, as also at $60.4 million due to a 2.1-fold increase in per capita rate, as well as at $7.5 million due to the rise in population. The average annual growth in government expenditure is 2.0%. The minimum value of government expenditure was in 1970 at $25.9 million. The maximum value of public expenditure was in 2010 at $916.6 million.

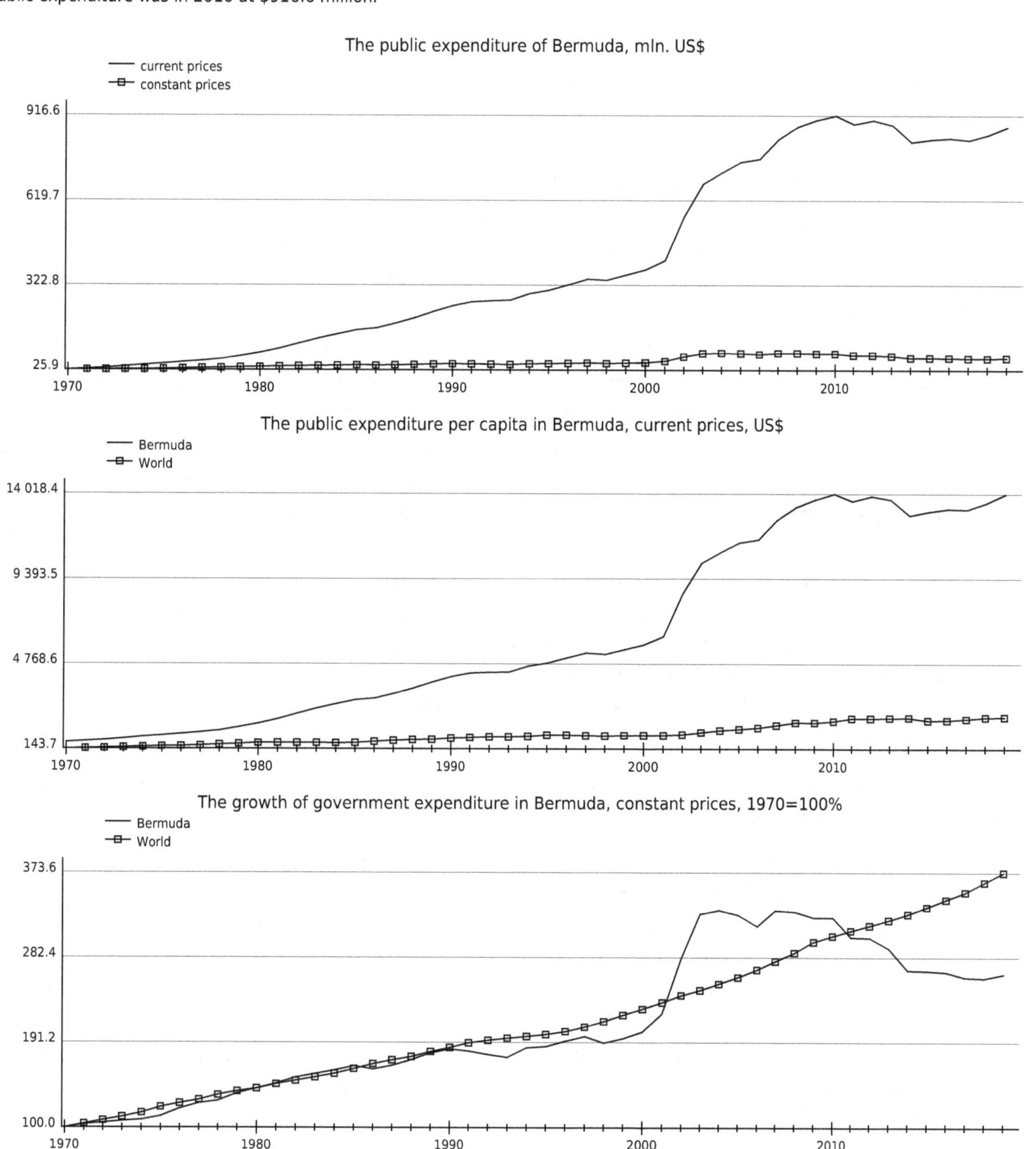

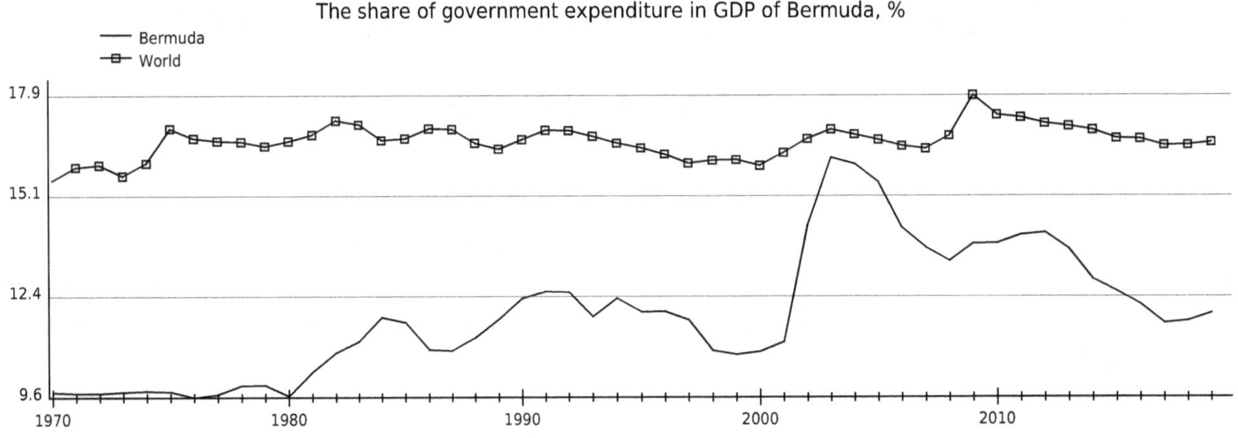

The share of government expenditure in GDP of Bermuda, %

The 1970s

The Bermuda's public expenditure was $46.7 million per year in the 1970s, ranked 144th in the world. The share in the world was 0.0044%, and 0.013% in the Americas.

The share of government consumption expenditure in GDP of Bermuda was 9.8% in the 1970s, ranked 157th in the world, and was on a par with Liechtenstein (9.8%), Turkey (9.8%), Switzerland (9.7%).

The government consumption expenditure per capita in Bermuda was $848.1 in the 1970s, ranked 29th in the world, and was on a par with the United Kingdom ($847.9), Austria ($847.4), Nauru ($845.4). The government expenditure per capita in Bermuda was greater than public expenditure per capita in the world ($265.2) in 3.2 times, and was greater than public expenditure per capita in the Americas ($655.5) by 29.4%.

The growth of public expenditure in Bermuda was 3.5% in the 1970s, ranked 136th in the world, and was on a par with Peru (3.5%), Nepal (3.5%), New Zealand (3.5%). The growth of government expenditure in Bermuda (3.5%) was less than growth of public expenditure in the world (3.7%), was greater than growth of government expenditure in the Americas (2.1%).

Comparison with neighbors. The Bermudian government consumption expenditure was less than in the United States ($285.9 billion) and in the Bahamas ($128.1 million). The government consumption expenditure per capita in Bermuda was greater than in the Bahamas ($683.5); but less than in the United States ($1 310.2). The growth of government consumption expenditure in Bermuda was greater than in the USA (0.94%) and in the Bahamas (0.27%).

Comparison with leaders. The Bermuda's government consumption expenditure was less than in the USA ($285.9 billion), in the USSR ($117.3 billion), in Germany ($95.6 billion), in Japan ($78.0 billion), and in France ($64.5 billion). The Bermudian public expenditure per capita was greater than in Japan ($700.2) and in the USSR ($465.0); but less than in the United States ($1 310.2), in Germany ($1 213.7), and in France ($1 202.3). The growth of government expenditure in Bermuda was greater than in the USA (0.94%); but less than in the USSR (7.2%), in Japan (5.3%), in France (5.0%), and in Germany (4.4%).

The 1980s

The government expenditure of Bermuda was $156.4 million per year in the 1980s, ranked 138th in the world. The share in the world was 0.0062%, and 0.018% in the Americas.

The share of government consumption expenditure in GDP of Bermuda was 11.1% in the 1980s, ranked 145th in the world, and was on a par with Brazil (11.2%), Somalia (11.2%), Argentina (11.0%).

The government expenditure per capita in Bermuda was $2 633.1 in the 1980s, ranked 24th in the world, and was on a par with Northern Europe ($2.6 thousand), Israel ($2.6 thousand), Germany ($2.6 thousand). The Bermudian public expenditure per capita was greater than government consumption expenditure per capita in the world ($523.5) in 5.0 times, and was greater than public expenditure per capita in the Americas ($1 287.2) in 2.0 times.

The growth of public expenditure in Bermuda was 2.8% in the 1980s, ranked 105th in the world. The growth of public expenditure in Bermuda (2.8%) was greater than growth of government expenditure in the world (2.7%), was greater than growth of public expenditure in the Americas (2.5%).

Comparison with neighbors. The Bermuda's government consumption expenditure was less than in the USA ($665.3 billion) and in the Bahamas ($425.2 million). The public expenditure per capita in Bermuda was greater than in the Bahamas ($1 834.9); but less than in the United States ($2.8 thousand). The growth of government consumption expenditure in Bermuda was greater than in the United States (2.6%) and in the Bahamas (1.3%).

Comparison with leaders. The Bermuda's government expenditure was less than in the USA ($665.3 billion), in Japan ($257.4 billion), in Germany ($203.7 billion), in the USSR ($181.1 billion), and in France ($159.8 billion). The public expenditure per capita in Bermuda was greater than in Germany ($2.6 thousand), in Japan ($2.1 thousand), and in the USSR ($658.0); but less than in France ($2.8 thousand) and in the USA ($2.8 thousand). The growth of government consumption expenditure in Bermuda was greater than in the USA (2.6%) and in Germany (0.98%); but less than in the USSR (5.4%), in Japan (3.5%), and in France (2.8%).

The 1990s

The Bermuda's government expenditure was $301.9 million per year in the 1990s, ranked 146th in the world, and was on a par with Barbados ($300.2 million), Fiji ($299.7 million). The share in the world was 0.0064%, and 0.020% in the Americas.

The share of government consumption expenditure in GDP of Bermuda was 11.8% in the 1990s, ranked 154th in the world, and was on a par with Liechtenstein (11.8%), Malaysia (11.8%), Switzerland (11.8%).

The government expenditure per capita in Bermuda was $4 775.4 in the 1990s, ranked 23rd in the world, and was on a par with Israel ($4.7 thousand). The government consumption expenditure per capita in Bermuda was greater than government consumption expenditure per capita in the world ($824.8) in 5.8 times, and was greater than public expenditure per capita in the Americas ($1 972.7) in 2.4 times.

The growth of government expenditure in Bermuda was 0.8% in the 1990s, ranked 137th in the world. The growth of government expenditure in Bermuda (0.82%) was less than growth of public expenditure in the world (2.0%), was less than growth of public expenditure in the Americas (1.1%).

Comparison with neighbors. The government expenditure of Bermuda was less than in the United States ($1.1 trillion) and in the Bahamas ($545.1 million). The public expenditure per capita in Bermuda was greater than in the United States ($4.3 thousand) and in the Bahamas ($1 970.4). The growth of government expenditure in Bermuda was less than in the United States (1.3%) and in the Bahamas (1.0%).

Comparison with leaders. The Bermuda's public expenditure was less than in the United States ($1.1 trillion), in Japan ($651.8 billion), in Germany ($419.6 billion), in France ($325.4 billion), and in the UK ($234.6 billion). The Bermudian public expenditure per capita was greater than in the USA ($4.3 thousand) and in the United Kingdom ($4.1 thousand); but less than in France ($5.5 thousand), in Germany ($5.2 thousand), and in Japan ($5.2 thousand). The growth of government consumption expenditure in Bermuda was less than in Japan (3.0%), in Germany (2.4%), in the United Kingdom (2.1%), in France (1.8%), and in the USA (1.3%).

The 2000s

The public expenditure of Bermuda was $687.1 million per year in the 2000s, ranked 141st in the world. The share in the world was 0.0088%, and 0.027% in the Americas.

The share of government expenditure in GDP of Bermuda was 14.0% in the 2000s, ranked 125th in the world, and was on a par with Uzbekistan (14.0%), Thailand (14.0%), China (14.0%).

The government expenditure per capita in Bermuda was $10 437.3 in the 2000s, ranked 8th in the world, and was on a par with Sweden ($10.3 thousand). The Bermuda's public expenditure per capita was greater than public expenditure per capita in the world ($1 200.9) in 8.7 times, and was greater than government expenditure per capita in the Americas ($2 931.6) in 3.6 times.

The growth of public expenditure in Bermuda was 5.2% in the 2000s, ranked 64th in the world, and was on a par with Eastern Africa (5.2%), Turkmenistan (5.2%), Asia (5.3%). The growth of public expenditure in Bermuda (5.2%) was greater than growth of public expenditure in the world (3.1%), was greater than growth of government consumption expenditure in the Americas (2.4%).

Comparison with neighbors. The Bermudian government expenditure was less than in the United States ($1.9 trillion) and in the Bahamas ($968.1 million). The government consumption expenditure per capita in Bermuda was greater than in the USA ($6.5 thousand) and in the Bahamas ($3.0 thousand). The growth of government expenditure in Bermuda was greater than in the USA (2.2%) and in the Bahamas (0.63%).

Comparison with leaders. The Bermudian government expenditure was less than in the USA ($1.9 trillion), in Japan ($844.2 billion), in Germany ($520.1 billion), in France ($479.9 billion), and in the UK ($453.4 billion). The Bermuda's public expenditure per capita was greater than in France ($7.6 thousand), in the United Kingdom ($7.5 thousand), in Japan ($6.6 thousand), in the United States ($6.5 thousand), and in Germany ($6.4 thousand). The growth of government consumption expenditure in Bermuda was greater than in the United Kingdom (2.9%), in the United States (2.2%), in Japan (1.7%), in France (1.7%), and in Germany (1.4%).

The 2010s

The government expenditure of Bermuda was $863.3 million per year in the 2010s, ranked 159th in the world, and was on a par with Fiji ($863.9 million), Mauritania ($856.5 million). The share in the world was 0.0066%, and 0.022% in the Americas.

The share of government consumption expenditure in GDP of Bermuda was 12.8% in the 2010s, ranked 159th in the world, and was on a par with Malaysia (12.8%), Mauritania (12.8%), the Bahamas (12.7%).

The Bermuda's government consumption expenditure per capita was $13 510.6 in the 2010s, ranked 9th in the world, and was on a par with Iceland ($13.8 thousand). The public expenditure per capita in Bermuda was greater than government expenditure per capita in the world ($1 785.1) in 7.6 times, and was greater than government consumption expenditure per capita in the Americas ($4 034.3) in 3.3 times.

The growth of government consumption expenditure in Bermuda was -2% in the 2010s, ranked 204th in the world. The growth of government expenditure in Bermuda (-2.0%) was less than growth of government expenditure in the world (2.3%), was less than growth of government expenditure in the Americas (0.45%).

Comparison with neighbors. The Bermudian government consumption expenditure was 3 073.4 times lower than in the United States ($2.7 trillion) and 41.1% lower than in the Bahamas ($1.5 billion). The Bermuda's government expenditure per capita was 62.7% higher than in the United States ($8.3 thousand) and 3.4 times higher than in the Bahamas ($3.9 thousand). The growth of government consumption expenditure in Bermuda was less than in the Bahamas (2.9%) and in the United States (0.0052%).

Comparison with leaders. The government expenditure of Bermuda was 3 073.4 times lower than in the USA ($2.7 trillion), 1 944.9 times lower than in China ($1.7 trillion), 1 208.1 times lower than in Japan ($1.0 trillion), 835.8 times lower than in Germany ($721.6 billion), and 738.9 times lower than in France ($637.9 billion). The Bermudian government expenditure per capita was 40.5% higher than in France ($9.6 thousand), 53.3% higher than in Germany ($8.8 thousand), 62.7% higher than in the United States ($8.3 thousand), 65.7% higher than in Japan ($8.2 thousand), and 11.3 times higher than in China ($1 197.3). The growth of government consumption expenditure in Bermuda was less than in China (8.3%), in Germany (1.9%), in Japan (1.3%), in France (1.3%), and in the United States (0.0052%).

Chapter XIII. Household consumption expenditure

(including Non-profit institutions serving households)

The Bermuda's household consumption expenditure grew up from $325.6 million per year in the 1970s to $3.3 billion per year in the 2010s, that is by $2.9 billion or 10.0 times. The change occurred at $2.7 billion due to a 5.8-fold increase in prices, as also at $180.1 million due to a 1.5-fold increase in per capita rate, as well as at $52.5 million due to the growth in population. The average annual growth in household consumption expenditure is 1.4%. The minimum value of household expenditure was in 1970 at $181.0 million. The maximum value of household expenditure was in 2019 at $3.5 billion.

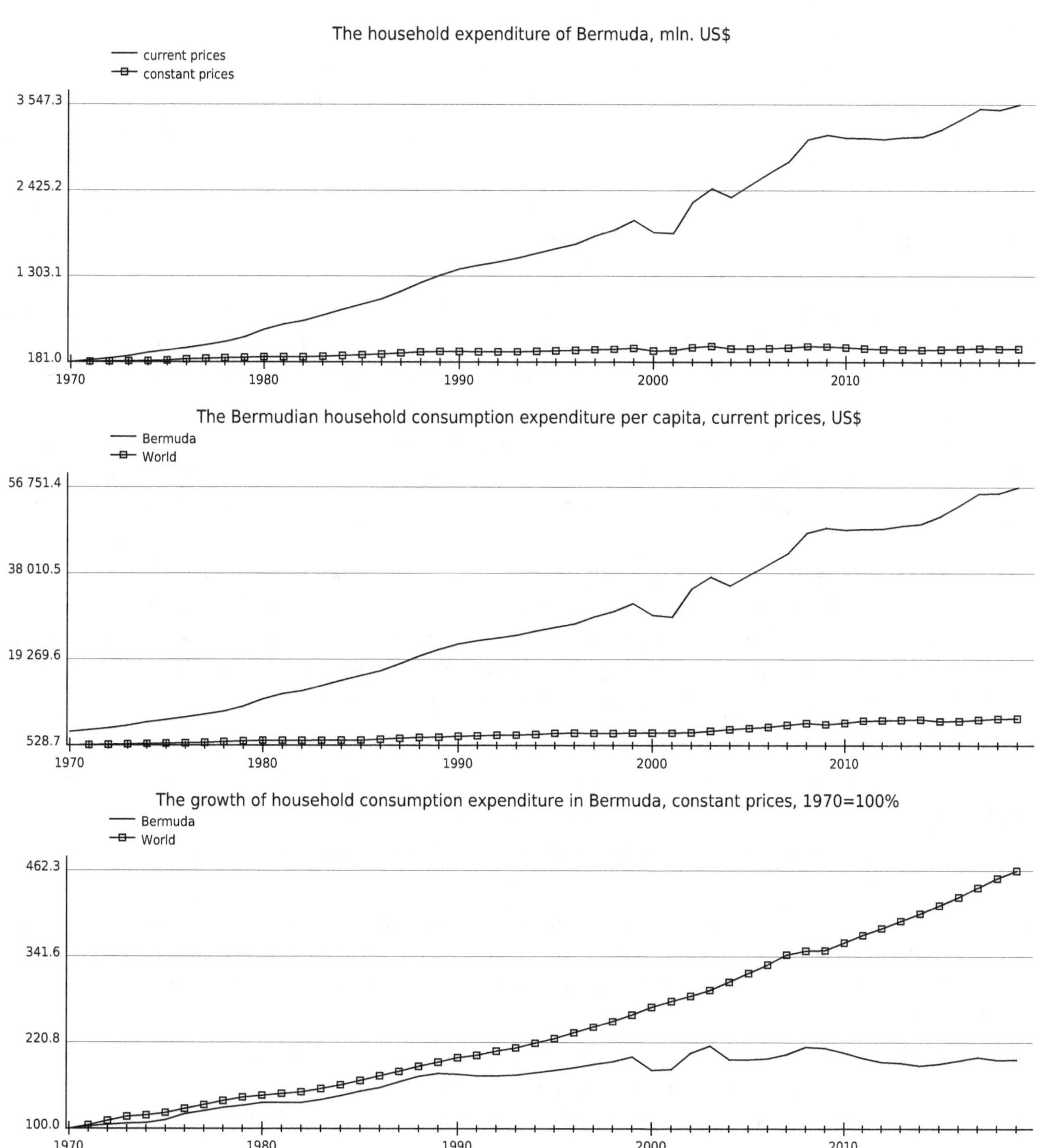

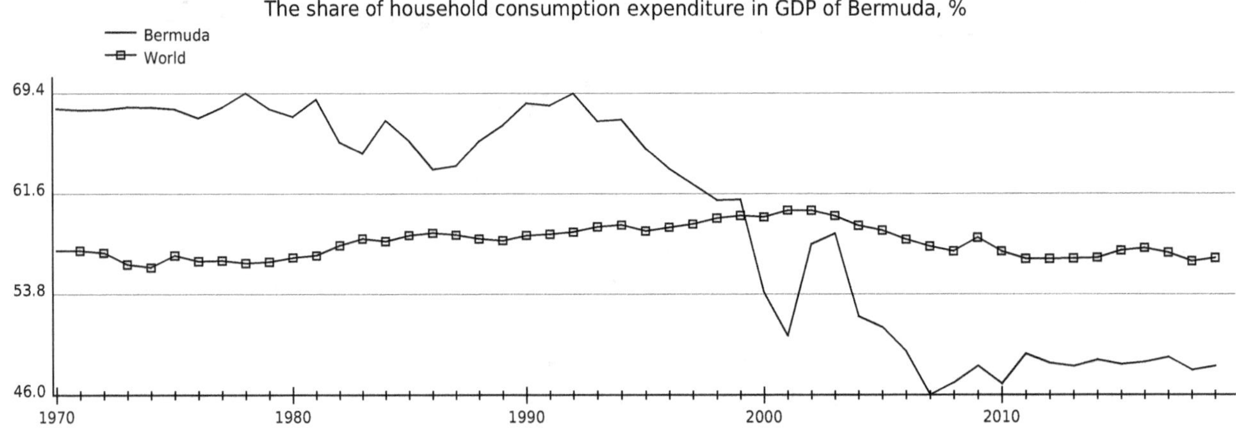

The 1970s

The Bermuda's household expenditure was $325.6 million per year in the 1970s, ranked 138th in the world, and was on a par with Suriname ($324.6 million), Fiji ($320.5 million). The share in the world was 0.0088%, and 0.024% in the Americas.

The share of household expenditure in GDP of Bermuda was 68.3% in the 1970s, ranked 76th in the world, and was on a par with Turkey (68.0%), Malawi (68.0%), Chile (68.6%).

The Bermuda's household expenditure per capita was $5 917.0 in the 1970s, ranked 3rd in the world. The Bermudian household consumption expenditure per capita was greater than household consumption expenditure per capita in the world ($914.8) in 6.5 times, and was greater than household consumption expenditure per capita in the Americas ($2 467.5) in 2.4 times.

The growth of household consumption expenditure in Bermuda was 3.1% in the 1970s, ranked 134th in the world, and was on a par with the Solomon Islands (3.1%), Senegal (3.2%). The growth of household consumption expenditure in Bermuda (3.1%) was less than growth of household consumption expenditure in the world (4.1%), was less than growth of household expenditure in the Americas (4.1%).

Comparison with neighbors. The household expenditure of Bermuda was less than in the USA ($1.0 trillion) and in the Bahamas ($588.3 million). The household consumption expenditure per capita in Bermuda was greater than in the USA ($4.7 thousand) and in the Bahamas ($3.1 thousand). The growth of household expenditure in Bermuda was less than in the USA (3.6%) and in the Bahamas (3.6%).

Comparison with leaders. The Bermudian household consumption expenditure was less than in the USA ($1.0 trillion), in the USSR ($310.6 billion), in Japan ($280.9 billion), in Germany ($277.8 billion), and in France ($180.7 billion). The household expenditure per capita in Bermuda was greater than in the United States ($4.7 thousand), in Germany ($3.5 thousand), in France ($3.4 thousand), in Japan ($2.5 thousand), and in the USSR ($1 231.6). The growth of household consumption expenditure in Bermuda was less than in Japan (5.1%), in the USSR (4.7%), in France (4.0%), in the USA (3.6%), and in Germany (3.6%).

The 1980s

The Bermudian household consumption expenditure was $925.5 million per year in the 1980s, ranked 129th in the world, and was on a par with Mauritius ($935.8 million). The share in the world was 0.011%, and 0.027% in the Americas.

The share of household consumption expenditure in GDP of Bermuda was 65.7% in the 1980s, ranked 87th in the world, and was on a par with Panama (65.8%), Turkey (65.8%), Iran (66.0%).

The household expenditure per capita in Bermuda was $15 580.6 in the 1980s, ranked 3rd in the world, and was on a par with the Cayman Islands ($15.3 thousand). The household consumption expenditure per capita in Bermuda was greater than household consumption expenditure per capita in the world ($1 808.0) in 8.6 times, and was greater than household expenditure per capita in the Americas ($5 090.2) in 3.1 times.

The growth of household expenditure in Bermuda was 3% in the 1980s, ranked 89th in the world, and was on a par with Jordan (2.9%), Syria (3.0%), Jamaica (3.0%). The growth of household expenditure in Bermuda (3.0%) was less than growth of household consumption expenditure in the world (3.0%), was greater than growth of household expenditure in the Americas (2.9%).

Comparison with neighbors. The household expenditure of Bermuda was less than in the United States ($2.6 trillion) and in the Bahamas ($1.5 billion). The household expenditure per capita in Bermuda was greater than in the United States ($10.9 thousand) and in the Bahamas ($6.4 thousand). The growth of household expenditure in Bermuda was less than in the Bahamas (7.4%) and in the United States (3.2%).

Comparison with leaders. The Bermuda's household consumption expenditure was less than in the USA ($2.6 trillion), in Japan ($945.6 billion), in Germany ($575.7 billion), in the USSR ($424.6 billion), and in the United Kingdom ($416.5 billion). The household expenditure per capita in Bermuda was greater than in the United States ($10.9 thousand), in Japan ($7.8 thousand), in Germany ($7.4 thousand), in the UK ($7.4 thousand), and in the USSR ($1 542.8). The growth of household consumption expenditure in Bermuda was greater than in Germany (1.8%); but less than in Japan (3.7%), in the UK (3.5%), in the USA (3.2%), and in the USSR (3.0%).

The 1990s

The household expenditure of Bermuda was $1.7 billion per year in the 1990s, ranked 143rd in the world, and was on a par with Botswana ($1.7 billion), Chad ($1.7 billion). The share in the world was 0.0098%, and 0.026% in the Americas.

The share of household expenditure in GDP of Bermuda was 64.9% in the 1990s, ranked 102nd in the world, and was on a par with India (64.9%), Portugal (64.8%), Northern Africa (64.7%).

The household consumption expenditure per capita in Bermuda was $26 303.8 in the 1990s, ranked 4th in the world. The household expenditure per capita in Bermuda was greater than household expenditure per capita in the world ($2 963.9) in 8.9 times, and was greater than household expenditure per capita in the Americas ($8 394.4) in 3.1 times.

The growth of household consumption expenditure in Bermuda was 1.2% in the 1990s, ranked 153rd in the world. The growth of household expenditure in Bermuda (1.2%) was less than growth of household consumption expenditure in the world (3.0%), was less than growth of household consumption expenditure in the Americas (3.3%).

Comparison with neighbors. The Bermuda's household expenditure was less than in the United States ($4.9 trillion) and in the Bahamas ($3.4 billion). The household consumption expenditure per capita in Bermuda was greater than in the United States ($18.5 thousand) and in the Bahamas ($12.1 thousand). The growth of household consumption expenditure in Bermuda was less than in the United States (3.4%) and in the Bahamas (3.2%).

Comparison with leaders. The Bermuda's household consumption expenditure was less than in the USA ($4.9 trillion), in Japan ($2.3 trillion), in Germany ($1.2 trillion), in the United Kingdom ($884.5 billion), and in France ($783.0 billion). The Bermudian household expenditure per capita was greater than in the United States ($18.5 thousand), in Japan ($18.2 thousand), in the UK ($15.3 thousand), in Germany ($15.2 thousand), and in France ($13.2 thousand). The growth of household expenditure in Bermuda was less than in the USA (3.4%), in the UK (2.8%), in Germany (2.1%), in Japan (1.8%), and in France (1.8%).

The 2000s

The Bermudian household expenditure was $2.5 billion per year in the 2000s, ranked 147th in the world. The share in the world was 0.0091%, and 0.023% in the Americas.

The share of household consumption expenditure in GDP of Bermuda was 50.7% in the 2000s, ranked 166th in the world, and was on a par with Belgium (50.8%), Eastern Asia (50.6%), Central Asia (51.1%).

The Bermuda's household consumption expenditure per capita was $37 918.6 in the 2000s, ranked 4th in the world. The Bermudian household expenditure per capita was greater than household consumption expenditure per capita in the world ($4 208.2) in 9.0 times, and was greater than household expenditure per capita in the Americas ($12 522.4) in 3.0 times.

The growth of household expenditure in Bermuda was 0.6% in the 2000s, ranked 196th in the world. The growth of household expenditure in Bermuda (0.60%) was less than growth of household consumption expenditure in the world (3.0%), was less than growth of household expenditure in the Americas (2.7%).

Comparison with neighbors. The Bermudian household expenditure was less than in the United States ($8.5 trillion) and in the Bahamas ($5.6 billion). The Bermuda's household consumption expenditure per capita was greater than in the USA ($28.8 thousand) and in the Bahamas ($17.4 thousand). The growth of household consumption expenditure in Bermuda was greater than in the Bahamas (0.19%); but less than in the USA (2.4%).

Comparison with leaders. The household consumption expenditure of Bermuda was less than in the USA ($8.5 trillion), in Japan ($2.6 trillion), in Germany ($1.5 trillion), in the United Kingdom ($1.5 trillion), and in France ($1.1 trillion). The Bermuda's household consumption expenditure per capita was greater than in the USA ($28.8 thousand), in the UK ($25.0 thousand), in Japan ($20.4 thousand), in Germany ($18.9 thousand), and in France ($18.1 thousand). The growth of household expenditure in Bermuda was greater than in Germany (0.46%); but less than in the USA (2.4%), in the United Kingdom (2.1%), in France (2.0%), and in Japan (0.81%).

The 2010s

The Bermudian household consumption expenditure was $3.3 billion per year in the 2010s, ranked 161st in the world, and was on a par with Liechtenstein ($3.3 billion), Guyana ($3.3 billion). The share in the world was 0.0074%, and 0.019% in the Americas.

The share of household consumption expenditure in GDP of Bermuda was 48.3% in the 2010s, ranked 177th in the world, and was on a par with Czechia (48.2%), Bhutan (48.5%), Central Asia (48.6%).

The Bermuda's household consumption expenditure per capita was $51 045.1 in the 2010s, ranked 3rd in the world. The household consumption expenditure per capita in Bermuda was greater than household consumption expenditure per capita in the world ($6 018.5) in 8.5 times, and was greater than household consumption expenditure per capita in the Americas ($17 389.9) in 2.9 times.

The growth of household consumption expenditure in Bermuda was -0.8% in the 2010s, ranked 200th in the world. The growth of household consumption expenditure in Bermuda (-0.79%) was less than growth of household consumption expenditure in the world (2.8%), was less than growth of household consumption expenditure in the Americas (2.2%).

Comparison with neighbors. The household consumption expenditure of Bermuda was 3 737.9 times lower than in the United States ($12.2 trillion) and 2.2 times lower than in the Bahamas ($7.2 billion). The Bermuda's household consumption expenditure per capita was 33.8% higher than in the USA ($38.2 thousand) and 2.6 times higher than in the Bahamas ($19.4 thousand). The growth of household expenditure in Bermuda was less than in the USA (2.4%) and in the Bahamas (1.2%).

Comparison with leaders. The Bermuda's household expenditure was 3 737.9 times lower than in the United States ($12.2 trillion), 1 204.7 times lower than in China ($3.9 trillion), 915.9 times lower than in Japan ($3.0 trillion), 600.4 times lower than in Germany ($2.0 trillion), and 546.3 times lower than in the United Kingdom ($1.8 trillion). The household consumption expenditure per capita in Bermuda was 33.8% higher than in the United States ($38.2 thousand), 87.9% higher than in the United Kingdom ($27.2 thousand), 2.1 times higher than in Germany ($23.9 thousand), 2.2 times higher than in Japan ($23.4 thousand), and 18.2 times higher than in China ($2.8 thousand). The growth of household consumption expenditure in Bermuda was less than in China (8.3%), in the USA (2.4%), in the UK (1.8%), in Germany (1.4%), and in Japan (0.64%).

Chapter XIV. Food consumption

During the research period the food consumption grew in spices (by 65.8%), vegetable oils (by 54.2%), vegetables (by 23.3% 18.2%), sugar (by 8.8%), meat (by 6.6%), but fell in cereals (by 9.9%), stimulants (by 13.4%), eggs (by 26.7%), fruits (by alcoholic beverages (by 33.9%), pulses (by 36.4%), treenuts (by 43.2%), milk (by 97.3%), starchy roots (by 98.9%).

These are the correlation coefficients between the GNI per capita in constant prices and the food consumption: vegetable oils (0.92 fish (0.807), spices (0.717), sugar (0.706), vegetables (-0.001), meat (-0.176), cereals (-0.495), fruits (-0.537), alcoholic beverages (-0.617), pulses (-0.796), stimulants (-0.798), treenuts (-0.82), eggs (-0.826), milk (-0.918), starchy roots (-0.932).

The 1970s

Kcal supply in Bermuda was 2 816.2 kcal/capita/day in the 1970s, ranked 41st in the world, and was on a par with Uruguay (2 823.4 kcal/capita/day), French Polynesia (2 831.2 kcal/capita/day), Kiribati (2 832.3 kcal/capita/day). Kcal supply in Bermuda was greater than in the world (2 403.2 kcal/capita/day), and was greater than in the Americas (2 754.7 kcal/capita/day). Structure of kcal supply: meat (19.2%), cereals (18.3%), sugar (12.8%), milk (8.7%), alcoholic beverages (6.9%), and others (34.1%).

Protein supply in Bermuda was 95.2 g/capita/day in the 1970s, ranked 19th in the world, and was on a par with Western Europe (95.3 g/capita/day), the Netherlands (94.9 g/capita/day), Canada (94.7 g/capita/day). Protein supply in Bermuda was greater than in the world (65.0 g/capita/day), and was greater than in the Americas (79.0 g/capita/day). Structure of protein supply: meat (36.6%), milk (17.9%), cereals (14.6%), fish (12.5%), vegetables (5.2%), and others (13.2%).

Fat supply in Bermuda was 122.7 g/capita/day in the 1970s, ranked 13th in the world, and was on a par with New Zealand (122.7 g/capita/day), Iceland (123.4 g/capita/day), the United States (121.9 g/capita/day). Fat supply in Bermuda was greater than in the world (55.1 g/capita/day), and was greater than in the Americas (85.8 g/capita/day). Structure of fat supply: meat (35.4%), vegetable oils (17%), milk (9.4%), stimulants (4.4%), cereals (4.2%), and others (29.6%).

These are the levels of food consumption in the world rankings: 7th - stimulants (8.2 kg/capita/yr), 8th - meat (99.1 kg/capita/yr), 11th - fish (38.2 kg/capita/yr), 12th - eggs (13.3 kg/capita/yr), 13th - fruits (139.6 kg/capita/yr), 14th - spices (1.5 kg/capita/yr), 21st - alcoholic beverages (92.5 kg/capita/yr), 22nd - milk (181.9 kg/capita/yr), 33rd - sugar (42.1 kg/capita/yr), 61st - vegetable oils (7.7 kg/capita/yr), 85th - starchy roots (38.4 kg/capita/yr), 123rd - pulses (1.7 kg/capita/yr), 138th - cereals (72.2 kg/capita/yr).

The 1980s

Kcal supply in Bermuda was 2 999.0 kcal/capita/day in the 1980s, ranked 40th in the world, and was on a par with Romania (3 004.2 kcal/capita/day), Canada (3 004.6 kcal/capita/day), South Korea (3 005.5 kcal/capita/day). Kcal supply in Bermuda was greater than in the world (2 572.3 kcal/capita/day), and was greater than in the Americas (2 917.7 kcal/capita/day). Structure of kcal supply: cereals (22.1%), meat (18.3%), sugar (10.9%), vegetable oils (8.4%), milk (7.7%), and others (32.6%).

Protein supply in Bermuda was 104.5 g/capita/day in the 1980s, ranked 11th in the world, and was on a par with Australasia (104.8 g/capita/day), Turkey (104.1 g/capita/day), the USSR (105.0 g/capita/day). Protein supply in Bermuda was greater than in the world (69.1 g/capita/day), and was greater than in the Americas (81.7 g/capita/day). Structure of protein supply: meat (35.9%), cereals (17.2%), milk (15.1%), fish (12.9%), vegetables (5.9%), and others (13%).

Fat supply in Bermuda was 128.8 g/capita/day in the 1980s, ranked 16th in the world, and was on a par with Finland (127.8 g/capita/day), Czechoslovakia (129.9 g/capita/day). Fat supply in Bermuda was greater than in the world (63.2 g/capita/day), and was greater than in the Americas (96.3 g/capita/day). Structure of fat supply: meat (33.5%), vegetable oils (22.1%), milk (9.5%), stimulants (5.5%), cereals (5.3%), and others (24.1%).

These are the levels of food consumption in the world rankings: 4th - meat (107.0 kg/capita/yr), 7th - eggs (16.1 kg/capita/yr), 8th - spices (2.4 kg/capita/yr), 10th - stimulants (9.4 kg/capita/yr), 11th - treenuts (4.5 kg/capita/yr), 12th - fish (43.3 kg/capita/yr), 17th - alcoholic beverages (107.2 kg/capita/yr), 20th - vegetables (130.1 kg/capita/yr), 22nd - fruits (126.3 kg/capita/yr), 32nd - milk (166.5 kg/capita/yr), 46th - sugar (38.7 kg/capita/yr), 54th - vegetable oils (10.6 kg/capita/yr), 96th - starchy roots (30.2 kg/capita/yr), 114th - cereals (93.8 kg/capita/yr), 126th - pulses (1.6 kg/capita/yr).

The 1990s

Kcal supply in Bermuda was 2 839.4 kcal/capita/day in the 1990s, ranked 53rd in the world, and was on a par with Kuwait (2 841.5

...a/day), Mauritius (2 832.9 kcal/capita/day), Brunei (2 826.2 kcal/capita/day). Kcal supply in Bermuda was greater than in the ...(2 652.6 kcal/capita/day), and was less than in the Americas (3 035.8 kcal/capita/day). Structure of kcal supply: cereals (20.2%), ...at (18.1%), sugar (12.2%), vegetable oils (8.6%), alcoholic beverages (7.4%), and others (33.5%).

Protein supply in Bermuda was 94.8 g/capita/day in the 1990s, ranked 31st in the world, and was on a par with the United Kingdom (95.0 g/capita/day), Estonia (95.5 g/capita/day). Protein supply in Bermuda was greater than in the world (72.1 g/capita/day), and was greater than in the Americas (86.2 g/capita/day). Structure of protein supply: meat (36.8%), cereals (15.2%), milk (12.5%), fish (12.4%), vegetables (8.1%), and others (15%).

Fat supply in Bermuda was 113.6 g/capita/day in the 1990s, ranked 26th in the world, and was on a par with Macao (114.3 g/capita/day), Samoa (114.3 g/capita/day). Fat supply in Bermuda was greater than in the world (69.0 g/capita/day), and was greater than in the Americas (100.9 g/capita/day). Structure of fat supply: meat (35.5%), vegetable oils (24.1%), milk (7.9%), cereals (7.8%), stimulants (4.7%), and others (20%).

These are the levels of food consumption in the world rankings: 7th - fruits (197.7 kg/capita/yr), 9th - meat (98.4 kg/capita/yr), 10th - spices (2.6 kg/capita/yr), 16th - fish (39.9 kg/capita/yr), 20th - treenuts (3.7 kg/capita/yr), 23rd - eggs (11.8 kg/capita/yr), 56th - milk (123.9 kg/capita/yr), 73rd - vegetable oils (10.1 kg/capita/yr), 110th - starchy roots (33.3 kg/capita/yr), 141st - pulses (1.5 kg/capita/yr), 162nd - cereals (71.3 kg/capita/yr).

The 2000s

Kcal supply in Bermuda was 2 594.5 kcal/capita/day in the 2000s, ranked 104th in the world, and was on a par with Western Africa (2 589.6 kcal/capita/day), Central Asia (2 589.0 kcal/capita/day), Suriname (2 602.1 kcal/capita/day). Kcal supply in Bermuda was less than in the world (2 765.9 kcal/capita/day), and was less than in the Americas (3 186.4 kcal/capita/day). Structure of kcal supply: cereals (22.2%), meat (18.8%), sugar (13.7%), vegetable oils (11.7%), alcoholic beverages (7.6%), and others (26%).

Protein supply in Bermuda was 83.5 g/capita/day in the 2000s, ranked 66th in the world, and was on a par with Chile (83.5 g/capita/day), Mauritius (83.7 g/capita/day), Brazil (83.9 g/capita/day). Protein supply in Bermuda was greater than in the world (76.5 g/capita/day), and was less than in the Americas (91.2 g/capita/day). Structure of protein supply: meat (40.7%), cereals (16.7%), fish (12.8%), milk (12.1%), vegetables (5.5%), and others (12.2%).

Fat supply in Bermuda was 112.4 g/capita/day in the 2000s, ranked 36th in the world, and was on a par with Cyprus (111.4 g/capita/day), the Americas (113.5 g/capita/day). Fat supply in Bermuda was greater than in the world (76.9 g/capita/day), and was less than in the Americas (113.5 g/capita/day). Structure of fat supply: meat (33.8%), vegetable oils (30.7%), cereals (9.5%), milk (7.2%), stimulants (3.5%), and others (15.3%).

These are the levels of food consumption in the world rankings: 13th - meat (94.8 kg/capita/yr), 14th - fish (44.0 kg/capita/yr), 25th - sugar (47.0 kg/capita/yr), 27th - alcoholic beverages (90.7 kg/capita/yr), 37th - stimulants (6.4 kg/capita/yr), 43rd - vegetables (114.7 kg/capita/yr), 46th - fruits (108.6 kg/capita/yr), 53rd - treenuts (2.1 kg/capita/yr), 63rd - eggs (7.8 kg/capita/yr), 77th - milk (104.7 kg/capita/yr), 139th - starchy roots (23.1 kg/capita/yr), 147th - pulses (1.5 kg/capita/yr), 168th - cereals (69.8 kg/capita/yr).

The 2010s

Kcal supply in Bermuda was 2 661.5 kcal/capita/day in the 2010s, ranked 108th in the world, and was on a par with Gambia (2 661.5 kcal/capita/day), Cyprus (2 660.8 kcal/capita/day), Panama (2 665.3 kcal/capita/day). Kcal supply in Bermuda was less than in the world (2 869.3 kcal/capita/day), and was less than in the Americas (3 219.3 kcal/capita/day). Structure of kcal supply: cereals (24.9%), meat (19.4%), sugar (13.2%), vegetable oils (10.9%), milk (5.1%), and others (26.5%).

Protein supply in Bermuda was 89.4 g/capita/day in the 2010s, ranked 57th in the world, and was on a par with Czechia (89.5 g/capita/day), Algeria (89.5 g/capita/day), Brunei (89.2 g/capita/day). Protein supply in Bermuda was greater than in the world (80.6 g/capita/day), and was less than in the Americas (92.7 g/capita/day). Structure of protein supply: meat (41.6%), cereals (16.5%), fish (13.8%), milk (10.1%), vegetables (5.7%), and others (12.3%).

Fat supply in Bermuda was 117.1 g/capita/day in the 2010s, ranked 39th in the world, and was on a par with Cyprus (117.6 g/capita/day), New Zealand (117.8 g/capita/day), Kuwait (116.1 g/capita/day). Fat supply in Bermuda was greater than in the world (82.4 g/capita/day), and was less than in the Americas (118.2 g/capita/day). Structure of fat supply: meat (33.7%), vegetable oils (27.8%), cereals (11.2%), milk (7%), stimulants (5%), and others (15.3%).

These are the levels of food consumption in the world rankings: 7th - meat (105.7 kg/capita/yr), 15th - fish (45.1 kg/capita/yr), 27th - spices (2.4 kg/capita/yr), 32nd - vegetables (130.5 kg/capita/yr), 33rd - sugar (45.8 kg/capita/yr), 37th - stimulants (7.3 kg/capita/yr), 44th - eggs (10.5 kg/capita/yr), 47th - fruits (106.9 kg/capita/yr), 49th - alcoholic beverages (69.1 kg/capita/yr), 60th - treenuts (2.3 kg/capita/yr), 73rd - vegetable oils (12.0 kg/capita/yr), 92nd - milk (92.2 kg/capita/yr), 147th - pulses (1.3 kg/capita/yr), 152nd - starchy roots (19.3 kg/capita/yr), 170th - cereals (65.7 kg/capita/yr).

Part V. Reproduction

Chapter XV. Gross fixed capital formation

(including Acquisitions less disposals of valuables)

The gross fixed capital formation of Bermuda increased from $67.3 million per year in the 1970s to $856.3 million per year in the 2010s, that is by $789.0 million or 12.7 times. The change occurred at $692.9 million due to a 5.2-fold increase in prices, as also at $85.3 million due to a 2.1-fold increase in per capita rate, as well as at $10.8 million due to the rise in population. The average annual growth in fixed capital formation is 2.5%. The minimum value of gross fixed capital formation was in 1970 at $37.3 million. The maximum value of gross fixed capital formation was in 2008 at $1.1 billion.

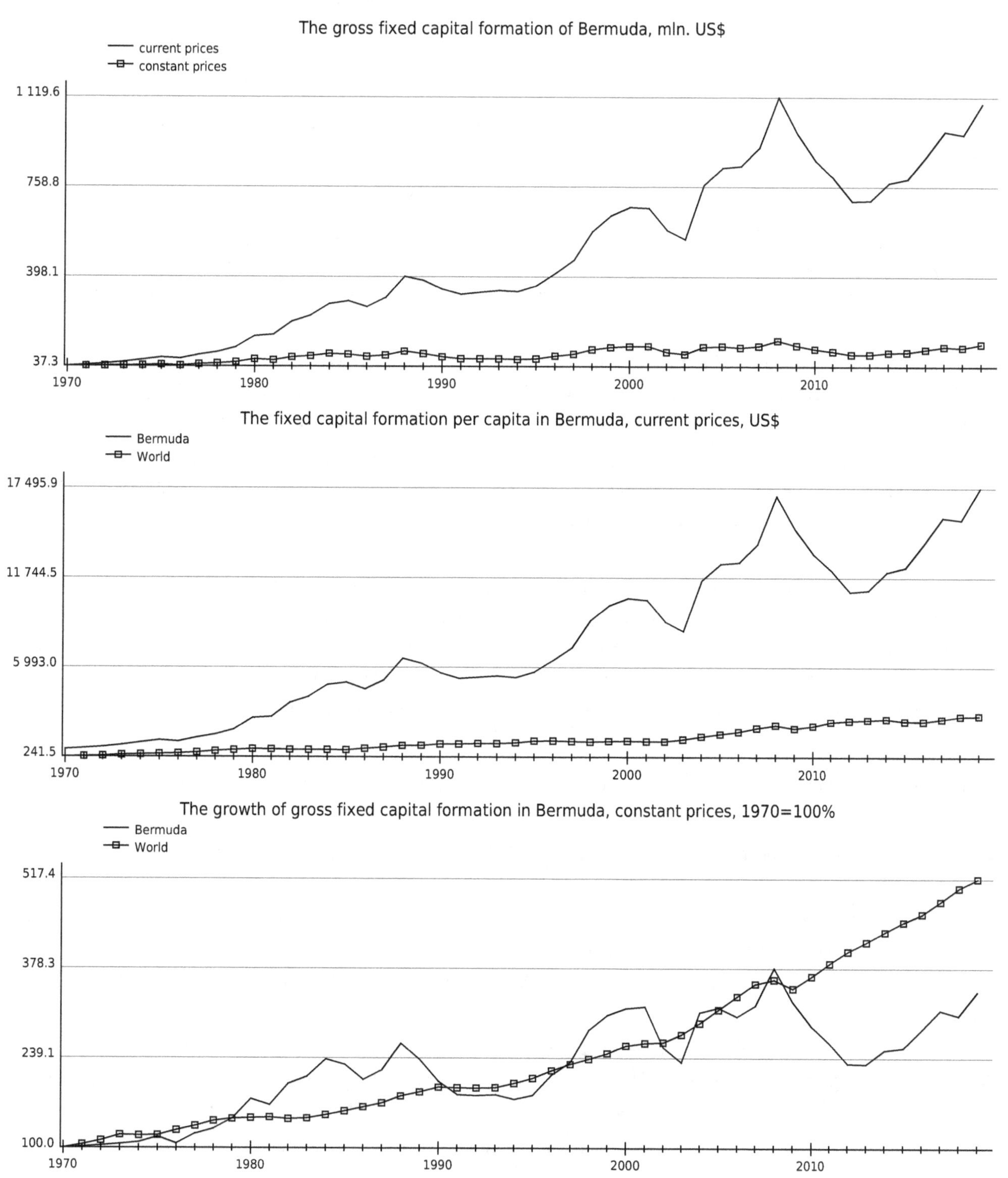

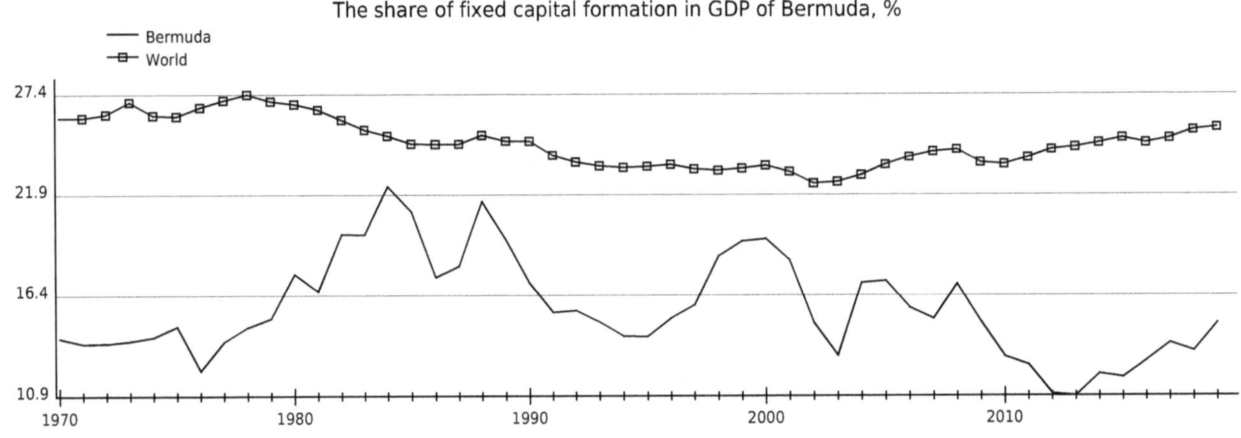

The share of fixed capital formation in GDP of Bermuda, %

The 1970s

The fixed capital formation of Bermuda was $67.3 million per year in the 1970s, ranked 144th in the world, and was on a par with Cambodia ($66.9 million). The share in the world was 0.0038%, and 0.013% in the Americas.

The share of gross fixed capital formation in GDP of Bermuda was 14.1% in the 1970s, ranked 156th in the world.

The fixed capital formation per capita in Bermuda was $1 222.3 in the 1970s, ranked 34th in the world, and was on a par with Aruba ($1 231.8), Nigeria ($1 240.6). The Bermuda's fixed capital formation per capita was greater than gross fixed capital formation per capita in the world ($433.5) in 2.8 times, and was greater than gross fixed capital formation per capita in the Americas ($913.4) by 33.8%.

The growth of fixed capital formation in Bermuda was 4.2% in the 1970s, ranked 113th in the world, and was on a par with Tanzania (4.2%), Albania (4.2%), the World (4.2%). The growth of fixed capital formation in Bermuda (4.2%) was less than growth of gross fixed capital formation in the world (4.2%), was less than growth of fixed capital formation in the Americas (5.3%).

Comparison with neighbors. The Bermuda's gross fixed capital formation was less than in the United States ($381.9 billion) and in the Bahamas ($239.9 million). The Bermuda's fixed capital formation per capita was less than in the USA ($1 750.0) and in the Bahamas ($1 280.0). The growth of fixed capital formation in Bermuda was greater than in the Bahamas (2.7%); but less than in the USA (4.4%).

Comparison with leaders. The Bermudian fixed capital formation was less than in the United States ($381.9 billion), in the USSR ($214.6 billion), in Japan ($191.6 billion), in Germany ($125.8 billion), and in France ($82.9 billion). The fixed capital formation per capita in Bermuda was greater than in the USSR ($850.9); but less than in the United States ($1 750.0), in Japan ($1 720.7), in Germany ($1 597.2), and in France ($1 545.4). The growth of gross fixed capital formation in Bermuda was greater than in Japan (3.9%), in the USSR (3.2%), in France (2.7%), and in Germany (1.5%); but less than in the USA (4.4%).

The 1980s

The Bermudian fixed capital formation was $273.9 million per year in the 1980s, ranked 127th in the world, and was on a par with El Salvador ($279.6 million), Liechtenstein ($268.2 million). The share in the world was 0.0072%, and 0.022% in the Americas.

The share of fixed capital formation in GDP of Bermuda was 19.5% in the 1980s, ranked 127th in the world, and was on a par with Mali (19.5%), Chile (19.6%), the Cook Islands (19.6%).

The Bermuda's gross fixed capital formation per capita was $4 611.6 in the 1980s, ranked 7th in the world, and was on a par with Sweden ($4.6 thousand), Japan ($4.7 thousand). The Bermudian gross fixed capital formation per capita was greater than gross fixed capital formation per capita in the world ($790.9) in 5.8 times, and was greater than fixed capital formation per capita in the Americas ($1 848.1) in 2.5 times.

The growth of gross fixed capital formation in Bermuda was 5% in the 1980s, ranked 48th in the world, and was on a par with Swaziland (5.0%), Australasia (5.0%). The growth of gross fixed capital formation in Bermuda (5.0%) was greater than growth of fixed capital formation in the world (2.5%), was greater than growth of gross fixed capital formation in the Americas (1.9%).

Comparison with neighbors. The gross fixed capital formation of Bermuda was less than in the United States ($958.4 billion) and in the

Bahamas ($657.7 million). The Bermudian gross fixed capital formation per capita was greater than in the United States ($4.0 thousand) and in the Bahamas ($2.8 thousand). The growth of fixed capital formation in Bermuda was greater than in the USA (3.1%); but less than in the Bahamas (14.3%).

Comparison with leaders. The fixed capital formation of Bermuda was less than in the USA ($958.4 billion), in Japan ($571.7 billion), in the USSR ($271.0 billion), in Germany ($238.1 billion), and in France ($164.3 billion). The gross fixed capital formation per capita in Bermuda was greater than in the United States ($4.0 thousand), in Germany ($3.1 thousand), in France ($2.9 thousand), and in the USSR ($984.8); but less than in Japan ($4.7 thousand). The growth of gross fixed capital formation in Bermuda was greater than in Japan (4.8%), in the USA (3.1%), in France (2.4%), in the USSR (1.7%), and in Germany (1.4%).

The 1990s

The Bermudian gross fixed capital formation was $415.0 million per year in the 1990s, ranked 146th in the world, and was on a par with Malawi ($423.7 million), Madagascar ($425.2 million). The share in the world was 0.0062%, and 0.020% in the Americas.

The share of gross fixed capital formation in GDP of Bermuda was 16.2% in the 1990s, ranked 173rd in the world, and was on a par with Puerto Rico (16.2%), Pakistan (16.1%), Kenya (16.1%).

The Bermuda's fixed capital formation per capita was $6 562.9 in the 1990s, ranked 14th in the world, and was on a par with Sweden ($6.6 thousand), the United Arab Emirates ($6.7 thousand), Germany ($6.5 thousand). The gross fixed capital formation per capita in Bermuda was greater than gross fixed capital formation per capita in the world ($1 183.8) in 5.5 times, and was greater than fixed capital formation per capita in the Americas ($2 694.1) in 2.4 times.

The growth of fixed capital formation in Bermuda was 2.6% in the 1990s, ranked 120th in the world, and was on a par with Burkina Faso (2.6%), Northern Africa (2.6%). The growth of gross fixed capital formation in Bermuda (2.6%) was less than growth of gross fixed capital formation in the world (2.8%), was less than growth of gross fixed capital formation in the Americas (4.4%).

Comparison with neighbors. The Bermudian fixed capital formation was less than in the United States ($1.6 trillion) and in the Bahamas ($1.3 billion). The gross fixed capital formation per capita in Bermuda was greater than in the USA ($6.1 thousand) and in the Bahamas ($4.7 thousand). The growth of gross fixed capital formation in Bermuda was less than in the Bahamas (5.1%) and in the USA (4.8%).

Comparison with leaders. The Bermudian gross fixed capital formation was less than in the USA ($1.6 trillion), in Japan ($1.3 trillion), in Germany ($520.7 billion), in France ($299.3 billion), and in the United Kingdom ($250.0 billion). The Bermuda's gross fixed capital formation per capita was greater than in Germany ($6.5 thousand), in the USA ($6.1 thousand), in France ($5.0 thousand), and in the United Kingdom ($4.3 thousand); but less than in Japan ($10.4 thousand). The growth of fixed capital formation in Bermuda was greater than in Germany (2.4%), in the United Kingdom (1.7%), in France (1.5%), and in Japan (0.18%); but less than in the USA (4.8%).

The 2000s

The Bermuda's gross fixed capital formation was $794.4 million per year in the 2000s, ranked 152nd in the world, and was on a par with Andorra ($779.7 million). The share in the world was 0.0072%, and 0.022% in the Americas.

The share of fixed capital formation in GDP of Bermuda was 16.1% in the 2000s, ranked 185th in the world.

The gross fixed capital formation per capita in Bermuda was $12 066.3 in the 2000s, ranked 10th in the world, and was on a par with Iceland ($12.2 thousand), Ireland ($12.2 thousand). The Bermudian fixed capital formation per capita was greater than gross fixed capital formation per capita in the world ($1 690.7) in 7.1 times, and was greater than fixed capital formation per capita in the Americas ($4 079.3) in 3.0 times.

The growth of fixed capital formation in Bermuda was 0.7% in the 2000s, ranked 171st in the world, and was on a par with the United Kingdom (0.66%), Northern America (0.66%). The growth of fixed capital formation in Bermuda (0.67%) was less than growth of gross fixed capital formation in the world (3.5%), was less than growth of fixed capital formation in the Americas (1.3%).

Comparison with neighbors. The fixed capital formation of Bermuda was less than in the USA ($2.8 trillion) and in the Bahamas ($2.5 billion). The Bermuda's fixed capital formation per capita was greater than in the United States ($9.4 thousand) and in the Bahamas ($7.8 thousand). The growth of gross fixed capital formation in Bermuda was greater than in the United States (0.43%); but less than in the Bahamas (1.8%).

Comparison with leaders. The gross fixed capital formation of Bermuda was less than in the United States ($2.8 trillion), in Japan ($1.2 trillion), in China ($1.0 trillion), in Germany ($557.7 billion), and in France ($463.9 billion). The gross fixed capital formation per capita in Bermuda was greater than in the USA ($9.4 thousand), in Japan ($9.0 thousand), in France ($7.4 thousand), in Germany ($6.9 thousand), and in China ($782.2). The growth of gross fixed capital formation in Bermuda was greater than in the USA (0.43%), in Germany (-0.56%), and in Japan (-2.0%); but less than in China (13.4%) and in France (1.6%).

The 2010s

The gross fixed capital formation of Bermuda was $856.3 million per year in the 2010s, ranked 164th in the world, and was on a par with Malawi ($869.7 million). The share in the world was 0.0045%, and 0.017% in the Americas.

The share of fixed capital formation in GDP of Bermuda was 12.7% in the 2010s, ranked 200th in the world, and was on a par with Eswatini (12.6%).

The Bermudian gross fixed capital formation per capita was $13 400.4 in the 2010s, ranked 12th in the world, and was on a par with Macao ($13.3 thousand), Sweden ($13.2 thousand), New Caledonia ($13.7 thousand). The Bermudian gross fixed capital formation per capita was greater than gross fixed capital formation per capita in the world ($2 621.1) in 5.1 times, and was greater than gross fixed capital formation per capita in the Americas ($5 284.2) in 2.5 times.

The growth of gross fixed capital formation in Bermuda was 0.5% in the 2010s, ranked 164th in the world. The growth of gross fixed capital formation in Bermuda (0.47%) was less than growth of fixed capital formation in the world (4.1%), was less than growth of fixed capital formation in the Americas (2.9%).

Comparison with neighbors. The Bermudian gross fixed capital formation was 4 203.1 times lower than in the United States ($3.6 trillion) and 3.6 times lower than in the Bahamas ($3.1 billion). The fixed capital formation per capita in Bermuda was 19.0% higher than in the USA ($11.3 thousand) and 62.4% higher than in the Bahamas ($8.3 thousand). The growth of fixed capital formation in Bermuda was less than in the United States (3.8%) and in the Bahamas (2.2%).

Comparison with leaders. The gross fixed capital formation of Bermuda was 5 281.8 times lower than in China ($4.5 trillion), 4 203.1 times lower than in the USA ($3.6 trillion), 1 413.3 times lower than in Japan ($1.2 trillion), 878.8 times lower than in Germany ($752.5 billion), and 813.7 times lower than in India ($696.8 billion). The fixed capital formation per capita in Bermuda was 19.0% higher than in the United States ($11.3 thousand), 41.7% higher than in Japan ($9.5 thousand), 45.8% higher than in Germany ($9.2 thousand), 4.2 times higher than in China ($3.2 thousand), and 25.0 times higher than in India ($535.2). The growth of gross fixed capital formation in Bermuda was less than in China (8.0%), in India (5.8%), in the USA (3.8%), in Germany (2.8%), and in Japan (1.8%).